WRITING THROUGH FEAR

PRAISE FOR CAROLINE DONAHUE AND THE STORY ARCANA GUIDES

Tarot isn't just for divination. In [the] *Story Arcana [Guides]*, Caroline Donahue shows how it can be the perfect muse for writing inspiration. Her clever methods and deep knowledge of Tarot will help break through blocks and get back to the business of writing. I predict you'll love this book and use it often.

THERESA REED, AUTHOR OF *TAROT: NO QUESTIONS ASKED - MASTERING THE ART OF INTUITIVE READING* AND *TAROT FOR TROUBLED TIMES*

Story Arcana [Guides are] a fresh take on the writing process that totally delighted me. I never thought of using tarot with writing before but now I see so many exciting possibilities! My writing process will never be the same. I've even used it with my writing clients and they're thrilled with the creative boost they get from the approach.

J. THORN, THEAUTHORLIFE.COM AND CO-AUTHOR, *THE THREE STORY METHOD*

Dive into the enchanting world of storytelling with Caroline Donahue's *Story Arcana* [*guides*]. Seamlessly blending the mystique of tarot with the art of crafting narratives, Donahue illuminates a path where creativity meets intuition. Through her insightful guidance, writers of all levels will uncover a treasure trove of inspiration, using tarot cards as literary allies to unlock plot twists, delve into character depths, and navigate the intricate landscapes of their stories. *Story Arcana* is a must-have companion for anyone seeking to infuse their writing process with magic and meaning.

SHERILYN DECTER, AUTHOR OF THE
*MOONSHINER MYSTERIES, RUM
RUNNER'S TRILOGY,* AND
BOOTLEGGER CHRONICLES

WRITING THROUGH FEAR

A STORY ARCANA GUIDE

CAROLINE DONAHUE

spree

The things we fear the most are often the things we should fear the least. It's irrational, but it's what makes us human. And if we're able to conquer those fears, then there's nothing we're not capable of.

T.J. KLUNE, *THE HOUSE IN THE CERULEAN SEA*

INTRODUCTION

When I wrote *The Author's Journey,* formerly released as *Story Arcana: Tarot for Writers,* I focused on the cycle of the first 22 cards in the tarot. The drama and adventure of the Major Arcana was enough to fill a book, and then some.

I never meant to stop after the first 22 cards, but until this past year it was unclear how to best share the next section of the tarot without simply repeating the same card interpretations that have already been written about in the many excellent books out there, most of which are sitting on my shelves now.

Since 2019, when my previous book came out, I've had the good fortune to teach an influx of writing students. Lockdown and the pandemic meant a dramatic increase in enrollment, and I saw many more stories and writers struggling through the challenges of getting a book on the page.

What struck me most was the difference between those students who achieved their goals, finishing drafts, finding agents, and moving into the publication process, versus those who froze at some point, never to reach THE END. I felt I'd somehow failed these students and I wanted to know what was keeping them from the complete draft they'd signed up for my course to write.

The answer to that question is the fears I've cataloged in this book. We all have a nasty little voice in our mind, a collection of doubts and negative beliefs we've picked up over our lives, called the inner critic. It tells us that we're not capable of finishing our books and that, even if we do get them written, no one in the world wants to read them.

The difference I witnessed over and over in class after class was that those who were able to overcome the critic's bullying were able to finish their books. Those who were hypnotized by its monologue in their mind stopped writing.

There are too many books hiding in your imagination that we need to have for this to continue. Every time one of my students told me the premise of their book, I couldn't wait to read it. I've been so honored to get to read several students' manuscripts, and every time is just as exciting as all the others.

Your book matters. And the fears that hold you back can be worked with so they don't shut you down. I started to see patterns in the fears among groups of students. Despite the critic whispering that you're the only one who has this issue, I assure you that you're not.

Fear comes in types, and this book reveals forty types of fear, matched up with the Ace through Ten in each of the four suits of the tarot: Cups, Wands, Swords, and Pentacles.

You don't need to be familiar with tarot to use this book. Tarot enthusiasts will be able to add their own associations to the cards I reference to add depth to these chapters, but that experience isn't necessary to benefit.

———

Understanding the fingerprint of the fears that stop you when you write is a gift to yourself as well as your future readers. The critic is a function of our psychology that was designed to keep us safe. It doesn't like us taking risks or doing anything unpredictable, much like adults don't want children running into the road. But writing a book isn't the same as dodging in front of a car, and you're no longer a small child. This choice is yours to make.

Getting clear about which messages are coming from the critic helps you clarify which concerns are, in fact, important ones: being respectful of and treating cultures other than your own sensitively and with respect is one example, particularly if you were raised with privilege. These are questions we need to consider without the critic running rampant in our minds.

Looking at ways to honor characters and their heritage is a question that needs your attention. Not being able to spell everything perfectly without spell check or to format dialogue without the assistance of a guide or editor doesn't mean you're not allowed to write.

I hope that the sections of this book will help you explore your fear deeper, becoming friends with it and seeing it as a helpful force in your writing, rather than a barrier to ever beginning.

How to use this book

Trust your instincts. If you're familiar with the tarot or have a deck available, try pulling a card and using the descriptions here to point you toward a fear to consider for the day.

You can work through the book from start to finish, answering the questions to ponder in a journal or however you prefer to reflect on them. Use these pages in a way that feels right to you.

In addition, don't skip over any fear that doesn't match one you have. Just because it isn't your own experience, considering unfamiliar fears could help with character development in the future. One of the first questions I ask when starting a novel is what the main characters' worst fears are. A lot of depth can come from this question, so remember this book is here for your characters' fears as well as your own.

Above all, remember that fear doesn't have to shut you down. It's sending up a flare that something doesn't feel right. Pay attention, but don't let it scare you away from writing at all.

Connecting to and understanding emotions more deeply is one of the gifts of being a writer. Maybe you didn't start writing as a psychological development process, but I have yet to find any other as effective at revealing our challenges and giving us the chance to work through them.

———

Pay attention to your reactions, go as slow as you need to, but keep coming back to the page. You've got this.

Caroline Donahue
    Berlin, Germany
    April 2024

CUPS OVERVIEW

WE BEGIN WITH THE EMOTIONS, since we are after all dealing with one of them: fear. It lives in the darkest depths of the ocean. The light is dim here, making it difficult to see what swims past us clearly. Our imaginations conjure terrors beyond what is actually there. But sometimes our fear is justified. Sometimes we risk life as we know it when diving this far below the surface.

I remember visiting the Baltimore Aquarium as a child, riding an escalator surrounded by strange clicking noises and sonar shrieks as we passed large pictures of fish. But these were unlike any fish I'd ever seen in a tank. They looked more like saber-toothed tigers with giant black unblinking black eyes and silver armor. They hypnotized me. I was terrified, yet I couldn't look away.

This is how fear claims us. You may try to discredit or ignore the fear that overtakes you when you approach writing. Your conscious mind may feel it's ridiculous to get scared, but it isn't. Your nervous system registers fear that lives in your imagination the same way it marks fear of dangerous things in the physical world. All fear is very real. It's only by treating it seriously that we can move past our resistance and anxiety toward writing.

The Cups contain these watery depths in symbolic vessels. We can peer down into our fears from a safe distance, feeling them in manageable sips before backing away to reflect.

As with all the suits we'll explore together, the Cups will show us a spectrum of experiences of fear. Not all of them look like sharp-toothed monsters in the dark. As you'll see, some of the fears that shut us down appear quite sunny on the surface. We'll be peering underneath and looking at the many kinds of webs we get tangled in when writing.

Know that not every fear will feel familiar. We have a fingerprint based on our own life experience and emotions. Some of these will connect to your experiences, and some won't. All these fears are worth exploring, if not for you then for your characters, who have emotional lives and challenges of their own to illustrate in your stories.

Set your ideas about how fear works aside, and let's sink below the surface of the water to find our first set of fears. Once we come back up, the ocean might feel more like a place you'd visit on purpose. At the very least, this tour will give you the tools you need to navigate the deep sea safely. Let's begin.

2

ACE OF CUPS

WHEN WE MAKE contact with a story that demands that we write it, feelings bubble to the surface. We care about this project, and caring inspires fear. In many ways, all the fear we have about writing boils down to this first one:

What if I invest in this project and it doesn't work out?

When we are scared to begin writing, the deeper concern is if it's safe to devote ourselves to an aspiration that might not succeed. This is a vulnerable place to be, and pretty much everything that matters to us in life requires a similar level of risk.

Starting anything new comes with risk. We might not thrive in a new job. The person we are in love with now might not feel the same way in the future. The worst fear lying underneath beginning for writers: Even if I devote myself to this book and write it as well as I can, even if everything goes according to my plan, one day I'll have to release control by sharing it. What will happen then?

As writers, we spend much of our time in our heads. We ponder language, and how we can express an idea eloquently, or spin a riveting tale that keeps the reader's eyes glued to the page. We learn how to lay out the structure of our project, striving to keep a neat and tidy grip on the arc that leads from start to finish.

I hate to break it to you, but writing gets messy. You won't necessarily be able to make an outline and peacefully type up the book without interruptions, doubts, or changes. Writing isn't about becoming a brain in a jar, either. We'll talk about the mind later in the book, but for now we remain with the heart, a place that can be scary for writers to hang out.

If you decide to write books, articles, or anything that you want others to read, the work will ask you to connect with your own emotions more deeply. You won't be able to circle around the hard parts. Writing means looking closely at the feelings many would rather avoid.

This isn't a hostage situation, however. You can pick and choose which emotional situations you write about, and sometimes it's wise to avoid those you find too distressing to dive into. What you can't avoid completely is emotion, period. If you want to write a book that means something to you and your future readers, you must connect with feelings, both your characters' and your own.

——

WHEN STARTING A BOOK, it's ok if you don't plummet to the emotion's oceanic bottom right from the start. Just like actual deep-sea diving, going too far down too quickly can be dangerous. Instead, submerge gradually to acclimate as you descend, keeping in mind that having feelings arise while writing is a normal part of the process, and ultimately one of the huge benefits of being a writer.

Ask yourself at the beginning if there's anything about your idea that feels too challenging to engage with emotionally. This is a question that can be useful to explore with a therapist or coach, especially when the topic feels too big to consider on your own. Many writers race into topics that bring up intense feelings without considering the impact on their own mental health, which can lead to distressing and painful consequences. You don't have to set an idea aside forever, but sometimes after assessing the intensity, waiting longer can prove to be the best choice.

You aren't required to write every idea immediately. If you've just been through a wrenching experience, it's not necessary to duplicate that exact situation with your characters, or to immediately write a memoir on that topic. If, upon reflection, the emotional content feels too raw, put time and space between you and this experience before using it for your writing.

You will have to feel when you write, so be aware of the feelings that serve your writing and those that compromise your mental health. As mentioned above, this is a delicate balance to strike. Having a second unbiased opinion in the form of a therapist or coach can make all the difference in these situations.

This isn't a clear-cut decision to make, and you may

have the sense that you're playing the childhood game I remember calling warmer/colder. You may need to use early drafts to approach an emotional element and see how involving this emotional material impacts the writing and you. Perhaps the writing is hugely satisfying, but you're a wreck every time you work on the project. That's a strong indication that it's best to step back, look for support, and ask if the same depth of emotion can happen in the book without using this precise path to get there.

Stories engage readers through emotion, so it does need to be present, but the way you weave in emotional themes can take an infinite number of forms. Let's look at how you can turn the volume down on content that proves too distressing for use right now.

AN EXAMPLE WILL HELP us clarify how this looks in practice. Let's say you're working on a novel and the main character has experienced a betrayal that shakes her tremendously and incites the arc that carries the remainder of the book. If you, the writer, begin working on this story with the Main Character (MC)having been cheated on by her spouse with a close friend, having been through the same thing yourself, keep a close watch on how you handle writing this story. It's possible this could be cathartic. But if you find it debilitating to write scenes that feel too close to home, you can change the content without sacrificing the emotion.

———

HOW ELSE CAN **we get here?**

This is one of my favorite exercises. Once you've set the above book aside because it's too triggering, take at least a day or two away from the story, and then try this journaling exercise:

First: clarify where the character needs to be as a result of this experience. Describe this without any reference to the situation, only to the emotional state your character is in.

Example from above: She feels betrayed, alone, abandoned, and like she can't trust anyone ever again. She feels like she was living a lie and that there is no way for her to feel confident going forward.

Write for at least five minutes to connect to the visceral experience of the emotion, but keep the level to a six or below on a scale of one to ten. Picture turning the volume down on the emotion or imagine the color fading from bright to more grayscale. If you're unable to adjust the emotional charge, this is not a suitable emotional theme to work on at this time. Stop the exercise and seek support before using this material again.

If you're able to safely engage the theme through the first exercise, set a timer again for five to ten minutes, listing every situation that pops into your mind that might land someone in that emotional state.

RETURNING TO OUR EXAMPLE:

· A friend backstabs the character to steal a promotion

at work, spreading gossip about the MC while pretending to support them getting the new role.

· The character discovers their mentor was secretly involved in an underhand business deal that goes against everything they appeared to stand for, and everything they taught your character.

· What examples can you imagine for this situation? Set a timer and practice, without the added weight of the emotional charge.

———

FREE-WRITING examples without judging or censoring for one timed round helps you generate as many alternatives as possible. If you're on a roll, continue on after the time is up. Once you feel complete, set the list aside until at least the next day. Then read through and ask yourself how the book would play out if each possibility was the experience the character had instead.

Sometimes one of these new situations will open you up to exploring the emotion more deeply, and in a way that won't cause you to suffer as you write.

We'll be exploring emotions and those fears connected to feelings and writing all through the Cups. It is possible to write without torturing yourself, so let's keep that as our guiding principle. And now, on to the Two.

QUESTIONS TO PONDER:

- What emotional themes feel too charged for me to write about at this point in my life?
- What support do I have currently, in the form of trusted family, friends, therapists, coaches, or other resources?
- What practices can I use to care for myself when difficult emotional themes emerge, such as journaling, arts activities, exercise, or meditation?
- How do I know when something is too much for me to engage with right now? What signs do I need to keep an eye out for that I've hit something too intense?

3

TWO OF CUPS

IRA GLASS, speaking about the creative process , shared an insight nearly all of us have read at one point:

"Nobody tells this to people who are beginners, I wish someone told me. All of us who do creative work, we get into it because we have good taste. But there is this gap. For the first couple years you make stuff, it's just not that good. It's trying to be good, it has potential, but it's not. But your taste, the thing that got you into the game, is still killer. And your taste is why your work disappoints you."

Usually, we get into writing because we love books. Perhaps you, like me, were up past your bedtime, sneaking more time to read. Stories provided a doorway into another world. It was, and is, magic.

The fear that tags along behind the love of books and

stories is the gnawing fear that nothing you write could ever measure up. Our taste, which as Ira Glass points out is killer, is never satisfied with the early shitty drafts we churn out in attempt after attempt to reach something divine.

THIS FEAR TAKES DIFFERENT FORMS. I had a client for whom it manifested as putting fiction on an impossibly high pedestal. She wrote beautiful nonfiction on a near-daily basis and was able to flow right into it, but as soon as her attention turned to the novel she'd been plotting in her head for years, the pedestal grew from the ground to so far up in the sky it was hidden by the clouds. Writing fiction felt more and more impossible the more special and different she felt that type of writing was.

When you start writing a book, the idea you carried in your mind is never translated exactly to the page. Often, it's unrecognizable compared to the feeling you are trying to convey. This hurts. You hear divine music in your ears and then write shrieking chords on the page and the distance between the two is nearly intolerable.

If we don't love our early drafts, it's easy to let the critic convince us that this is as good as they'll ever get. If you don't love it now, you'll never write anything you're happy with. And it's true to an extent that the completed book almost never looks the way you originally envisioned, but usually by that point it's taken a new form that feels more real, more subtle, and more complete.

It's easy to look at the first draft, or even the first several drafts, as a test. You've had an idea for a book, and the initial writing is meant to confirm if it "works." Looking at your first efforts as something to judge as worth continuing or not is unfair to both you and the book, as it is nowhere near fully formed at this stage. Early drafts are called rough drafts for a reason.

LET'S go back in time for a moment. How did you feel about taking tests? Even as a card-carrying nerd who enjoyed being in school, I never loved exams. The pressure to deliver my best work on someone else's timeline never felt right. My grades were good, but once I finished school I realized that this system didn't work well for me. I needed to work through several drafts at a more thoughtful pace to create writing that resonated. Even if you thrive under the pressure of a deadline, I suspect you also sometimes feel frustrated by this method, knowing the work could have been better without being yanked away at an often arbitrary point.

HERE'S what I propose as an alternative: don't judge your early drafts. When we remove the pressure to create the story we fell in love with immediately, it gives us the breathing room to explore and develop it before putting on the finishing touches of polished language and additional detail. Personally, I prefer to take the first draft or two to clarify what the story includes, confirming who the characters really are, what they want, and how I want to tell the story. This period of exploration is necessary, and without it I never feel I've gotten to the heart of the book.

Once I have written the story so I understand it myself, I then move to the question of how I want to share it with the reader. The structure of the novel may change once I have these elements clear for myself, and that's when things start to light up and feel exciting.

How would it feel not to have to prove your idea was worth working on by writing a perfect first draft?

Do you feel a sense of relief, of permission? Does this give you some breathing room? Or do things start to fall flat?

You might not agree with this approach. I know writers who work very differently and who love to revise as they go, polishing language and story simultaneously. As always, trust your instincts. The shift that makes you feel more connected to your work is the one that's right for you.

In my experience, books are a bit like the Ugly Duckling: they look nothing like their completed selves when you first hatch them out of their shells onto the page. But the appearance of the baby swan has no bearing on who it will grow to become. Nor does your first draft define your ultimate finished book.

WHEN WE EXPECT PERFECTION IMMEDIATELY, like we were trained to attempt to create in school, we forget about the possibility of revision. If we break the word apart, it isn't just an editing process, it's a new vision, hence the idea of "re-vision."

We have the chance to see the story and the book again before it leaves our hands and our control. Every time you do another pass on your book, you can adjust your vision. Early on, these may be big changes. Characters may combine, disappear, or new ones may leap into being. Someone who seemed minor may claim a larger role, and where the story begins and ends can vary widely. This is all part of the process.

What we have to learn to love is the potential of the idea, and we need to trust that we can put the work in to make it wonderful, even if we have no proof at all that this is possible. Love the exploration and the process but don't expect yourself to be perfect at the beginning.

Rilke put this better than I can, in one of the sections of *Letters to a Young Poet* I've held onto ever since I first read it. I can't think of better guidance for any novelist, unsure if the book will ultimately become the dream the writer envisioned:

"Be patient toward all that is unsolved in your heart and try to love the questions themselves, like locked rooms and like books that are now written in a very foreign tongue. Do not now seek the answers, which cannot be given you because you would not be able to live them. And the point is, to live everything. Live the questions now. Perhaps you will then gradually, without noticing it, live along some distant day into the answer."

If you can love the experience of possibility and the process of forming a book from potential, you stand to feel much more satisfied in your early drafts. Rather than living your way to the answer, you can draft your way from possible form to final manuscript, a process that can delight us as much as future readers if we allow ourselves the luxury of uncertainty throughout.

4

THREE OF CUPS

WHEN IN THE early stages of working on a book, I will do almost anything to avoid talking about it. Once you call yourself a writer, people want to know two things: have you written anything they might have read and what you're working on now. Before an idea forms completely, it's incredibly easy to get sucked into the mire by the fear that other people won't get what you're trying to do.

Building momentum to write a whole book requires tremendous investment in the story and in ourselves. The possibility of our book delighting others is part of the reason we go through the effort of writing it. But what if it falls flat?

I admit that I've had fantasies of reading excerpts from my as yet uncompleted novels at book release parties hosted by my favorite bookshops around the world. Having helped to set up and run many such events during my time working for a prominent bookstore in LA, I have all the details clear in my mind. Champagne might be my own fantasy, but I have definitely attended events with wine afterward, so it feels like a reasonable addition.

THE DESIRE TO reach this point is one of the most consistent dreams I hear about from writers. The details may vary from person to person: perhaps one writer longs for a particular sort of review, while another wants to see a reader on a plane, glued to their book, but overall we all want to feel our book is a success, the toast of the town.

The fear that hides behind this desire is that our book will flop. Perhaps no agent wants to take it, if we wish to publish traditionally. Or perhaps no publisher wants it even if an agent does. Or perhaps the book comes out as an indie or even with a well-known press and the champagne cork never pops. What we fear above all is that our book doesn't connect with the readers we dreamed would love it.

The inner critic will threaten you with this fear from the first day you sit down to write. What if no one cares about this book, it asks. What if you put all this effort in for nothing? The critic hates nothing more than wasted time and inefficiency, but it has a funny way of measuring these.

These objections are actually two very different consequences of working on a book that doesn't get the result you want. What if, as the critic suggests, no one cares about this book? This is a very tricky thing to measure. My first question is: what does no one caring about this book look like in your mind?

. . .

IN THE WORLD OF PUBLISHING, the window to become the sort of bestseller you see in newspaper and other lists is quite small. To get on the charts upon release means a huge amount of press has gotten people pre-ordering the book months before it comes out. This can also be the case for authors who've built up a devoted readership over time. Those readers just need to know there's a new book coming and they'll buy it with no further encouragement needed.

But this takes time. We see the books that are all over the media on most-anticipated or must-read lists and set that as our measure of success. We want to be "the book of the summer" or chosen for a celebrity book club among other accolades. It's so important to remember this is far from the only example of making an impact, and that in many cases, the impact can come long after initial publication.

I RECENTLY SPOTTED a book by Oliver Burkeman in a favorite bookshop that I hadn't heard about. Having loved his previous book, *Four Thousand Weeks*, I snatched it up, curious about why I hadn't heard about this new title. I flipped to the publication details and found the answer. It originally came out years ago, before the success of Burkeman's more recent book. The publisher had updated the cover and released a new edition, knowing that those who loved *Four Thousand Weeks* would now be hungry for more of his writing.

What if Oliver Burkeman had told himself that writing another book was pointless because that early book didn't create the buzz he'd hoped for? We might never have had the chance to read more of his work, which has made a tremendous difference to readers in recent years.

This is far from the only example. Jojo Moyes wrote multiple novels, most just modest successes before *Me Before You* exploded, catapulting her whole catalog onto the bestseller lists. I had the exact same experience as with Burkeman's book, thinking I'd found a new Jojo Moyes on the front display table at Powell's in Portland. Flipping it open, I learned this "new" book was actually part of her re-released backlist, now sporting the familiar design of *Me Before You's* cover.

The publishing industry rarely knows which book will be a hit. This happens in film as well, with smaller productions taking over the box office seemingly out of nowhere. Finding the right book for the collective mood in the world at that moment is a delicate, fiddly process. When we tighten the window down to a few weeks or a month after a book comes out as the only point when we measure success, we're doing the book — and ourselves — a tremendous disservice.

EXAMPLES ABOUND from other creative fields as well. Nick Drake wrote beautiful music that gathered only a modest audience during his lifetime, a source of much disappointment and suffering to him, understandably. I often wish he could have lived to see his songs reach millions in film soundtracks and played by fans around the world. I once asked to learn one of his songs when I took guitar lessons briefly in college, only to have my teacher laugh and shake his head. His chords are so complex and masterful that even professional musicians struggle to determine exactly how he played them. So was his music a flop, just because it wasn't universally celebrated the moment his first album came out? I don't think so.

As writers, we face many obstacles to our goals. Some of them are internal, in the form of the fears we'll explore through this book. Those we can work on reframing and overcoming. However, it's essential to remember that some obstacles are entirely out of our control. The more you restrict your definition of success, the harder it is to reach. For example, if you will only feel successful if you get a particular agent at a specific agency and get a publishing deal with the publisher you've wanted since you were little, this is going to be a tough slog. It also puts success entirely in other people's hands.

The antidote to this fear, I have found, is to think like a time traveler. My approach to my books is to write ideas I want to share with people and to work to publish them in ways that readers can find them from now into the future. Perhaps if the idea has showed up at a time that wasn't an exact match, the book and I can be patient, and then celebrate when readers find it in the future.

And in the meantime, we can all keep on writing.

5

FOUR OF CUPS

WRITING projects often begin in a flurry of excitement. The idea feels bright and shiny in our minds, but as soon as you start making notes, fear sets in. You wobble. What if this is a mistake? What if this idea isn't as brilliant as you thought it was?

The Four of Cups is the fear of disappointment. You feel the distance between the perfection of the idea as you first felt it and the imperfect reality as you attempt to nail it on the page. The shine slips off the idea and you may doubt it's worth writing this at all. Once again, we feel the gap between our ideal, our taste, and the actual text as we've written it.

This fear is based on a fundamental belief many writers get trapped by: that the quality of the idea determines the outcome of the writing project. If it's a "good idea," then the book will turn out well, and if the book doesn't turn out well, then the fault is with the original concept. Paired with the fear that we have no clue what we're doing, it's easy to spiral.

. . .

IF WE LOOK DEEPER, we can see that the obsession with the idea is completely misguided. Books begin with an idea, but if that was the sum total of their value, why would anyone bother with reading actual books? We'd just browse in bookshops, walking away having just consumed the back cover text, satisfied by that alone. But we don't. The idea may hook us, but that's what the concept of a book is supposed to do. Once we know what it's about, we're able to decide if we want to read it. It's reading that allows us to connect with the depth of the story.

Why would there be so many books in the world if the premise were the sole purpose? No one would bother writing full novels if no one ever read them. Plus, we wouldn't revisit the same concepts over and over — we'd have one book about people who met, fell in love, then perhaps disagreed and parted, only to find each other again in the end. Maybe there'd be a second book where the lovers don't end up together, and a few varieties for different sexual orientations and cultural backgrounds, but then that genre would be finished. But is it?

THE TRUTH IS the point of a story isn't the idea or the premise. Of course there are books that feel unique on multiple levels, but there are plenty more that don't. People who enjoy a certain premise as readers finish a book they love and immediately want to read more, right?

We don't read something that lights us up and say,

"Great! I've checked off Science Fiction now, so I never need to read an epic space opera again." We are already running to the library, the bookshop, or the internet to fill the loss we feel now that the book is over. (At least that's what this reader does.)

This moves us on to the next layer of this fear. If you accept that the idea being good enough isn't what your disappointment is about, you then realize that you're worried about being unable to do it justice. A feeling swept over you when you knew you wanted to write this book and now you've got some scratchings that feel nothing like that idea. What if your writing doesn't encapsulate the emotion you felt in a way the reader can also feel? What if the emotion is lost in the telling? What if the idea isn't a problem at all, but your writing is?

DISAPPOINTMENT IS part of the writing process, and unfortunately for writers, it's front-loaded. The difference between the idea and the draft is the largest when you begin writing and gets closer and closer to what you hoped it would be the more rounds you go through. However, you need to be prepared for the inevitable drift. The idea evolves as you write, so the book will change as you immerse yourself in the actual writing. The final project rarely resembles what first appeared in your imagination.

The sooner you understand this as part of the process and not a failure on your part, the easier it will be to engage with this experience with curiosity rather than fear. Writing isn't inert and stories don't have one final form they are destined to take. It's more like a snapshot. Who you are in the moment you have the idea mixes with who you become in the process of writing it, and the story itself transforms alongside both. Just like the tides of the ocean, there are cycles of change. The idea ripens, as does the writing itself. You're following a living narrative that has a cycle of growth. Think of a tree blooming rather than a blueprint that needs to be built exactly to spec.

All you need is the impulse to begin and an open mind for all the story can become. Rather than bracing yourself for disappointment, what if you opened yourself up for surprise? Being able to execute an exact copy of an idea existence in your head as a work on paper is no measure of your ability. It's an impossible task, just like the text of a menu can never recreate the flavor and texture of the food it describes. Writing is a guide that allows your reader to take their own journey through the textural map you've created, lighting up their own experience in their imaginations. Every reader's interpretation will be different, and the writer must surrender control of how it will be received.

What if this felt exciting rather than disappointing?

QUESTIONS TO PONDER

- What disappointment are you most afraid of when committing your story to the page?
- If you embrace this disappointment as inevitable, how does the fear shift, if at all?

- What happens if you imagine the final draft as a surprise that might be better than your original idea?
- If you could trust that the first draft was in no way reflective of what the ultimate book would look like, how would that shift your fear?

6

FIVE OF CUPS

WHEN WORKING ON A LARGE PROJECT, especially when revising, I find it feels like trying to get a squid into a suit. Large manuscripts, especially book-length ones like novels, are impossible to hold in your head all at once. They're floppy. When you try to get your mental arms around the whole piece, it resists. You want it to be neat and tidy, slipping into the trousers and buttoned up in a jacket and tie, but it Just. Won't. Fit.

Whenever I've worked on foundational aspects of a project, it feels like improving one area makes all the other areas worse. It's maddening. Perhaps I solve the character's backstory, only to realize this changes the time when the book took place. Or changing their career means moving the location to an entirely different setting.

ONE ASPECT not working perfectly isn't a reflection on the viability of your project, even though it often feels that way. When we see one discrete problem and think it's a structure disaster, we have landed on the Five of Cups fear.

In most images of this card, a figure faces toward two spilled cups but doesn't notice there are two behind them, still full. Boiled down, this is the catastrophizing card. Having unanswered questions about your book, even late in the game, doesn't mean you will never figure them out. It also doesn't mean you are a terrible writer, have a defective idea, an unworkable plot, character, or that everything is hopeless.

This fear tends to strike when you've been working hard and ignoring other needs, especially biological ones. An overstretched schedule plus a desire to write can lead us to cut sleep, thinking that something has to give, but when we do that, fears like this one tend to appear.

If I've had a bout of insomnia, the first thing to suffer is my belief in myself and my project. Lack of sleep makes everything look unsolvable. When you dive into your project and want to throw your computer out the window instead of working on it ever again, the following checklist is essential:

- Have I been sleeping well lately? If not, how many rough or short nights of sleep have I had in the last week?
- When was the last time I did something for fun? (If you can't remember, even if you have no other items of concern on this list, you'll need to follow the "refill your cups" protocol below.)

- Are there other stressful events happening in my life currently? (How many? List them.)
- How is my health right now? How is everyone I live with's health currently?
- What am I reading at the moment? Am I excited to read it?

IF ANSWERING these questions reminds you of pressure, health concerns or other stress, lack of sleep, fun, or leaving the house, or being completely uninspired by your current reading, it's time for the Five of Cups fear cure:

———

REFILL **Your Cups Emergency Protocol**

Follow these steps to replenish your creative self when it feels like all your writing effort has been for nothing. If you recognized any of the items in the checklist as a concern, the protocol will help. If multiple items rang a bell, taking these steps is urgent.

1. Stop reading your current book. Set it aside. Pick something else that feels incredibly indulgent and delicious. It should be the reading equivalent of your favorite meal or holiday destination.

2. Cancel as many plans as possible. Go to bed as early as humanly possible. When we have demanding

schedules, we often stay up late to preserve time for ourselves. Your spare time needs to focus on sleep for at least a few days.

3. Call in some lazy points. Order food in or make frozen options if you are the cook for your family. See if you can let some chores slide for a little bit so you have some breathing room.

4. Take a break from writing and focus on refilling the well instead. This will depend on your preferred methods but options include:

- Watching a show you enjoy but is silly and a waste of time

- Getting in pajamas early in the evening

- Reading as many indulgent books as you want until you feel topped up.

- Watching films at home or going to the cinema

- A bookstore or library visit to pick out a juicy stack of reading

- Journaling that won't go in the book that can be messy

- Taking things slowly

- Connecting with a supportive writing friend, community, or mentor

APPLYING these steps can be a challenge, depending on your work, family, and life situation. When you have a newborn baby, things are going to look very different than for someone whose kids have left home. Those in a new job early in their careers will have different amounts of time than someone who's retired or on a sabbatical.

Within the life that you have, see if you can dial down the optional activities that drain you and take more time for rest. When we're tired or on the edge of burnout, we get scared that all might be lost. Once we're actually burned out, we stop caring entirely. Take it seriously if you are afraid there's no way to solve this project. There's always a solution. The question is if you want to put the effort in to find it. It's absolutely ok if the answer is no. However, that decision needs to be made when you're rested enough to think clearly.

When we fear all is for nothing, the image of this card is a helpful one to reflect on. Yes, some of the cups have been spilled, but more remain safe and undisturbed, you simply can't see them right now. By replenishing your creative inspiration as well as your physical energy level, the tunnel vision will widen so you can see the picture more clearly. In addition, getting support from others you trust can help show you that things are much better than they looked.

As for that squid you're trying to get into the suit, expand your idea of what success looks like, and the suit will get a lot larger and easier for your story to wiggle right into place. Every squid needs a custom suit — no book is one-size-fits-all.

COMPLETING A MANUSCRIPT TAKES TIME, but you will finish and publish it if you stay the course. After interviewing hundreds of authors for the podcast, I have yet to have someone tell me they wish their book had taken longer to write. But nearly all of them say that it worked out that they needed all the time it did take to finish a book they were proud of.

Focus on what's working, even if it's hard to see. Refill your cups when they feel low and you'll have the emotional reserves to see you through to THE END.

QUESTIONS TO PONDER:

- What sections can you break your book into to make it feel less ungainly in your mind?
- What are you pleased with about the project at the moment?
- Which books do you love, especially those you kind of hope no one knows you love reading?
- How much rest have you been getting lately?
- Which plans are optional on your calendar — can you reduce your commitments?

7

SIX OF CUPS

WRITE WHAT YOU KNOW. We've all heard this advice. On the whole, I find it useful. Applying your own experience to the stories you tell makes them feel more genuine, engaging readers more deeply. I've often told myself and my students that there are no bad days, only good material, but the truth is they can feel like bad days for quite a long time before we are ready to use them as material.

Even if we give ourselves ample time to process charged content, as discussed earlier in the Cups, writing what we know can still give rise fear. Students often confess the concern that their writing is too close to their actual life. Here they are following the advice to write what they know, but is it too revealing?

The Six of Cups is a card that speaks to nostalgia and an idyllic time in the past, usually childhood. The fear it invites us to understand is the challenge of using our memories in our work, particularly memories other people in our lives might recall quite differently. How much writing what we know is too much?

THIS IS A TRICKY LINE, and one that every writer has to assess for themselves. On the one hand, we have a writer like David Sedaris, who writes overt memoir, whose family assumes anything they say could show up in a book. They aren't wrong. But on the other hand, we have writers who are pulling from their own emotional experiences and infusing them into stories that are set in different times and worlds, so we'll never know what was connected to their actual lives and what is pure imagination. A difficult breakup could become a power struggle between world powers in a space opera. An unkind teacher can become a villain mastermind. It's possible to use relationship dynamics you've been part of without airing the laundry of the actual relationship.

When we take writing what we know too literally, then this fear becomes understandably intense. If you've grown up in a family where multiple members struggled with substance abuse and then think that's all you're allowed to write about, then of course you're going to worry about upsetting your family. However, expand the context in which that experience arises and you have many other options to work with. A character struggling against a monster they can't control, say, or shift the family dynamic from parent-child to siblings, friends, partners, or put it into a work setting with similar power dynamics. Spin the kaleidoscope of options and there are many ways to work with this personal material without identifying its source.

MANY TIMES, this experience happens from the opposite direction. We have an idea that appears entirely fictional, but partway through we realize a storyline or character feels extremely familiar. Then the fear appears. Is the person who exists out in the world going to recognize themselves in this book? This fear can shut people down, causing them to discard the entire concept.

This is what I always tell clients and students in the grip of this fear: write the early draft entirely for yourself. Use the material freely. Make it really obvious who you're referencing if that experience feels necessary or cathartic. Then revise to adjust or conceal before you share the book. If you avoid the chance to write as you originally envisioned, it does a disservice to yourself and the story.

Depending on the relationship, some people have also waited to write the book until the person in question is no longer alive, if that feels like the safest choice. This spares the concern about someone feeling hurt or exposed by your writing. This isn't the only way to be respectful toward others, though, given there are many options to reference your original experience.

I FIND that using the internal emotional experience to bring depth to a scene is most useful to me. If a character is accused of lying, then I can pull on hurtful experiences when someone didn't trust my word without bringing in the specifics of the situation. The emotional content makes the scene believable. Perhaps someone reading might wonder if I've ever had a similar experience since the scene felt true to them, but they wouldn't be able to figure out when or with whom this happened. With fiction, I find this the safest way to go. However, you'll need to consider the specifics of your situation to decide. Take it slowly, and explore multiple options, seeing how each one lands with you.

PERHAPS THE DYNAMICS in a relationship form the map of the character dynamics you want to share, but you're afraid the person you're referencing will recognize themselves in the story. I find that it's easier to assuage this fear if you change the surface details so that they will be less likely to draw a parallel, even if they read your book. I once pulled from an unpleasant dynamic in a dating relationship to help me paint a difficult father-daughter relationship, given that my relationship with my dad bears no resemblance to the one I was writing. However, the jumpiness my character felt, the fear she'd say the wrong thing and set off her father came from real life for me, just from an ex. When you shift the roles like this, people are less likely to notice.

This was a foundation-level choice in the project, so it wouldn't have worked to write the whole thing with the characters as partners and then shift it to a father-daughter relationship. Ask yourself what you're comfortable with at each stage of the process. When you're planning the book, writing, revising, and when you're ready to put it out in the world, you can check again to be sure.

We tend to believe that our innermost thoughts are broadcast with a megaphone when the book comes out, but people bring their own experiences and references to reading. The view we have of another person in our lives doesn't always match their self-concept. Perhaps a critical teacher we reference thought she was giving tough love. The teacher is unlikely to see themselves in a role they don't believe they were playing.

TRUST the story to carry you. The more we let characters diverge from their source material, the more they become their own people who have less need of the reference we built them on. Even if perhaps we had some notes about people we know or knew early on, whoever the people you are writing about are will become clear the more time you spend with them. As a result, this fear tends to be strongest in the first draft. We feel the most conceptual then, when the story and characters haven't fully formed in our minds.

As with new friends, the more time we spend with our characters, the more hidden depths they reveal. The more we learn about them in the context of the story, the more they will take on their own identities, which will often prove more different than their inspiration than we originally thought was possible.

. . .

TWYLA THARP'S wonderful book *The Creative Habit* revealed a key part of her process: when she first conceives of a dance, she has an image or story she thinks of as scaffolding for the choreography process. Perhaps it's even a story we know well, like Romeo and Juliet or a classic fairy tale. This holds the concept of the dance up as she creates it. But, in the end, the scaffolding comes down and the dance exists on its own. Tharp rarely shares the original inspiration for a piece because it doesn't matter once it's finished. No one could name it based on watching the dance alone. This reference was just the temporary container Tharp needed to crystallize the idea. I believe our memories and experiences are like this with writing.

By allowing ourselves to use what we know, we can bring depth of meaning and resonance to our writing that wouldn't otherwise be available, but once we infuse our energy and effort into the story, draft after draft, all that remains is the story itself. This is the magic of writing.

QUESTIONS TO PONDER:

- What if you trusted that where you draw inspiration from can be concealed so readers don't spot it?
- Would you feel more comfortable drawing from real-life experience if it served as a jumping-off point that was meant to change?
- What memories or experiences do you wish you could work with in your writing?

- What areas of your life are off-limits entirely,
  if any?

8

SEVEN OF CUPS

"WHAT'S THAT OVER THERE? I see it off in the distance... is it? Is it perhaps a better idea?"

Welcome to the Seven of Cups, the highly distracting shiny object syndrome. The fear most closely connected to this card is the fear of missing out on writing something way more fun.

"What if the idea I committed to isn't the best one I could have picked?" Even more insidious than worrying you want to write a different project is the endless FOMO that can appear inside the project you are writing. Like a Choose Your Own Adventure story gone wrong, every crossroads creates anxiety. Every choice you need to make is fraught.

What if I get this wrong?

The Seven of Cups fear is built on the same foundation as most other fears: the belief that there is a correct way to write your book. We will see this theme again and again throughout the cycle of fears. As long as you subscribe to the idea that there is one right answer, the fear of going the wrong way will hold you hostage.

What if there was no wrong way? Underneath the fear of going the wrong way is a much deeper fear: that of letting go of the other possibilities. It can feel quite delicious to have an array of ideas and possibilities laid out in front of you like a story buffet. Why wouldn't you want to have a little taste of all of them?

WHEN I WAS ABOUT to turn eight, I had an existential crisis. Yes, I started thinking like a writer early. Getting ready for my bath in my grandmother's house, it struck me that not only was I going to get older on my birthday the next day, everyone else was getting older, too including my mother, dad, grandmother, and everyone I knew. I stewed in the tub with this fear until I came up with the sort of solution a kid could understand.

"I'm not going to turn eight tomorrow," I announced to my mother, who was soaping up one of my grandma's monogrammed washcloths. If I stopped getting older, everyone else would stay the same age, too.

I presented this with such gusto that everyone went along with it. This pause in time calmed many of my age-related fears. In addition to everyone getting older, I had calculated that one day I would die without having read every book that had ever been written. There were new books appearing in shops all the time. We didn't even have the internet yet, as this was the mid-eighties, and I was already freaked out. There was no way I could get through the stacks of everything I wanted to read — even at seven I was already behind.

My family existed in a bubble where time froze until my younger brother (who was nearly five) slipped up and told another kid as we played, "You can't beat my sister. She's eight!" I decided that it was ok to be eight if it meant I was allowed to win at games, something I'd rarely managed before that.

This didn't solve the worry about all the books out there until I had the epiphany that not being able to read every book in the world meant I was allowed to skip the boring ones. This, I could live with.

Having to commit to your story is like this. We can't write every single possibility that could exist in one book. If you tried, you'd be writing the same book forever. In order to bring one idea to life, we have to say no to many others. Some of them may find a home in another project or another story, but some of them won't.

THIS NEVER FEELS EASY. You'll be able to let go of the options that feel wrong right away with less trouble, but that leaves an array of options that remain enticing. Remember that you're not deciding which one is the very best eternally. The one you choose doesn't have to stand towering over the others. They might both look equally shiny. You only need to choose the one that feels more enticing for you right now.

The longer we stay in one place staring at potential choices, the more likely we are to stagnate. Story is like a shark in this way: it needs to keep moving to breathe and live. Don't let the fear of making the wrong choice pin you in place, where your book will suffocate. Pick one of the Cups and move forward, working with what you have. Choose the adventure you want to have with this book, knowing that this will allow you more time to write others. Most of all, remember there is no perfect answer. You can only be the writer that exists right now in this moment. The you of the future might choose differently, but that doesn't make the choice you make now wrong.

AUTHOR ALEXIS HALL, writing in the new edition foreword of *Glitterland*, his first published novel, put it this way:

"Because I relentlessly second-guess myself, I can't quite tell the best tone to strike when talking about an early work. If I imply that I've got better since, it suggests the book you've just paid money for isn't as good as another one you could have chosen to purchase. If I imply I haven't, then that suggests I've spent the past decade stagnating creatively. Although actually, I think 'better' is a somewhat pointless term when you're talking about art in general (and, God, I find it difficult to refer to my own books as 'art'). Ultimately, every-thing is a combination of contexts. I don't think I could write Glitterland today, but I couldn't have written the book I'm currently working on a

decade ago and wouldn't be able to write it a decade from now either.

I kind of like that, though. It means every book you write (or, for that matter, read) has its own place in time."

THE BEST YOU can ask of yourself is to make the difficult choice of one Cup with a shiny treat inside. You can't have them all right now, but by not choosing at all, you end up with none, because the story can't progress. The more you surrender to the fact that choosing is a necessary part of the process, the easier it will be to choose in the future.

Making the best choice you can isn't easy. You're not doing it wrong if you feel unsure. It's hard to let possibilities go. But you're strong enough to do it. Trust your gut, even if it feels wobbly. The choice you make today is the one that suits the writer you are now. This is enough.

QUESTIONS TO PONDER:

- What distractions are most likely to suck you in?
- Changing character details?
- Shifting critical moments in the plot?
- Chucking the whole book and starting fresh?

- Is there a container you can create to capture other shiny ideas to refer back to later? This might be a journal, a blank document you can add to, voice notes on your phone, or a notes app.
- How can you catalog your shiny distractions, so they can provide inspiration at a later point?

9

EIGHT OF CUPS

SOMETIMES, a project no longer fits and the writer decides it's time to let it go. Rachael Stephen discussed this painful process when she came on the Secret Library Podcast.

Having written her first novel, she took on an ambitious project for her second, with complex plot lines and deep emotional themes. However, after wrestling with it for a few years, she came to a surprising conclusion: she didn't want to work on it anymore.

This is a tricky point, because it's very easy for the critic to hijack the impulse to stop. Rachael didn't fear working on the book, nor did she think she wasn't capable of finishing it, she simply no longer wanted to. The emotional place she was in when the idea first appeared was too different from the space she was in several years later and she felt trapped by the project.

The Eight of Cups is the moment we realize we want to walk away from the story and move on to something else. Wow, is this a point that can provoke fear. Up to this point, the critic may have been yelling that you can't do it, but as soon as you think of letting the book go, that same critic starts yelling about how you'll be a failure if you stop.

OUR CULTURE CELEBRATES PERSEVERANCE. In many cases this is a good thing, but not always. "Winners never quit," "No pain, no gain," and other slogans blasted across posters meant to motivate can have the opposite effect when the project no longer works.

Rachael ultimately decided that staying in the emotional space required to write the book was doing more harm than good, and she let it go. She felt immense relief as soon as she made the decision. This is an essential point to clarify: do you feel grief and disappointment if you contemplate stopping, or do you feel relief and freedom? It's important to understand whether you're walking away because of fear, or because you're trusting your instincts.

WHEN I WAS in my mid-twenties and working as a psychotherapist-in-training, something wasn't sitting well with me. I suspect now that at 24, I was too young to handle the pressure of that work, but despite that, I was good at it. However, every weekend I lay in a lump on the sofa, barely able to spend time on activities that I had previously enjoyed, because I was so depleted. In the moment I enjoyed it, but afterward I paid the price with a ravaged nervous system and symptoms of depression.

It was a huge struggle to decide what to do. I'd invested three years of my life and the tuition into a Master's Degree in Psychology. I'd made a plan to become a Jungian Analyst, which required getting a license and committing to many more years of study. But here I was, half-comatose only partway to my goal. After confessing my doubts to my supervisors, one of them gave me a piece of advice I've used to navigate tricky decisions ever since:

You'll know you're on the right path when you're moving toward something you want, not running away from something you don't.

———

WHEN WE GET scared about our ability to write a book, it's tempting to run away. We think a different idea might work better, or perhaps taking a class would help. Anything to get rid of the doubt. But running away from this feeling only gives you a brief pause. As soon as you find another idea, there the fear is again. Because the book isn't the problem in this case: it's the fear that we're incapable of writing it that's shutting us down.

On the other hand, if we start writing a book, like Rachael did, that's grounded in a particular time in our lives, perhaps a time when we were in a painful place, and writing it requires us to stay in that place, our desire to change projects feels different. I suspect this may have happened for some writers with ideas they began in lockdown. Whereas writing a book about feeling trapped and unable to live freely might have felt exactly right in 2020 and 2021, once we got to 2022 and beyond, that idea might have been more constricting than the writer was able to manage.

In this case, I suspect the desire to leave the idea behind felt more like wanting to write something more expansive in tone. Perhaps wanting to write a grand adventure rather than something based on confinement, be that emotional or physical. The cramped narrative is causing continued pain, even after its origin is no longer our reality.

This is a big difference. In the second case, you're getting an intuitive hit that a different project is a better choice, while in the first case you're scrambling to escape due to lack of faith in yourself.

BEING able to tell the difference between your intuition and your critic's voice is a big part of clarifying why you want to let a project go. In my experience, the critic uses a lot of words. It has no shortage of vocabulary and will spout it at you in torrents. It feels like a shrill monologue.

"Well, you know this is too much for you, what if you tried something simpler? You can't have all these characters running around all the time, how are you supposed to remember all the details? People won't understand what you're doing and it will be confusing. It was a nice try but better to change it. You don't want to look stupid, do you?"

. . .

BY CONTRAST, intuiting uses far fewer words. Nor does it threaten you with humiliation as the consequence of not following its advice. It's quieter, and sometimes the critic drowns it out.

"Hmmm. What about this?"

Hearing your intuition takes practice. The critic tends to get louder and more insistent when intuition shows up, hoping you'll miss the quieter voice's message. Intuition has the potential to make big things happen, and the critic is very afraid of this.

There's no need to make a decision quickly, if you suspect your project might no longer be working for you. You can take time to see how it feels if you let it go. If you're unsure, taking a break can often be a good test. And there's no requirement that you destroy the project just because you set it aside. Sometimes it's a question of "not now" rather than "not ever."

As always, journaling can be illuminating. Write about what you would do if you set this project aside for now. How would it feel? Unless you're under contract with a publisher, the decision is entirely yours. And even then, speaking to an editor about reimagining the project is often a possibility, depending on how close you are to deadline.

ASK questions and explore the answers. Only in certain circumstances are you required to finish this book if it's no longer right for you to do so. This doesn't make you a failure, or someone who's no longer a writer.

Many successful writers have let books go. Michael

Chabon generously shared a draft of a novel he ulti-mately chose not to finish, publishing a fragment of the novel in McSweeny's Issue 36 along with his commen-tary about what went wrong. Sadly, it's very difficult to get hold of this issue, as it's an incredible resource. I take comfort simply knowing it exists, and in Chabon's generosity in sharing publicly that this does indeed happen to authors deep into successful careers.

By understanding your fears around walking away from your project, you'll get clear about why you're drawn to this choice. Only you know what's right, but by listening closely, you'll find a choice that works for you, be that continuing with the book or choosing another story.

QUESTIONS TO PONDER:

- Have you ever let go of an idea?
- What do you think led to setting it aside?
- How might you handle this experience differently now?
- What does your critic think about letting projects go?
- Are there any projects you've set aside in the past that you want to return to now?
- What messages have you received about stopping projects before completion?

10

NINE OF CUPS

"BE CAREFUL WHAT YOU WISH FOR..." The strange warning we've heard since we were little wreaks its own havoc in the land of writing fear. While the Nine of Cups represents wishes fulfilled, this is by no means a simple outcome.

Despite dreaming of writing a book for years, it can feel daunting to check that life goal off. Will it be as satisfying as we imagined? Will reality measure up to the experience we created in our heads? Sometimes it feels more terrifying to find out what a wish coming true really feels like than to keep it as an unfulfilled dream.

For years, I dreamt of moving abroad. Ever since I was little, I wanted to live somewhere I had to speak another language. Not having taken advantage of a semester or year abroad during my education, this dream lingered. When my husband and I decided to move to Germany, arriving in 2018, I was exhilarated for the first few months. Finally, this dream had come true. But after a year or two, I realized how much the longing to achieve this goal had become part of my identity. Now that I'd gotten my wish, what was I meant to do next? It felt strange to cross that item off the list not having another dream of equal weight to replace it.

WITH WRITING, the fear of making a big splash with a book is that we won't have anything else to work toward afterward. Yes, there's always another book, but if we look at writing and publishing a book as a similar goal to running a marathon, say, once we've completed it there isn't anywhere to go next. We've done what previously felt impossible. How could just doing it again feel anywhere near as meaningful? This is the trouble with "someday" wishes and dreams: much of their value comes from their not having come true yet, while remaining tantalizingly just out of reach.

In addition, fears can arise because of accomplishing a goal. Once we'd moved to Berlin, I spent a lot of time afraid we wouldn't get work visas and then would have to move back. I was anxiety-ridden up until the moment we were granted our first two-year residency permits. Fears around achieving writing dreams can range anywhere from unexpected side effects of success to that success being snatched away once it has arrived.

In my more self-aware moments I've found the fears of side effects from writing success hilarious. Before Berlin, I lived in Los Angeles for twelve years, and I can't think of anything more awful than being famous enough to be recognized visually. This very rarely happens to writers, but my critic has jumped on this fear regardless, reminding me that if I keep writing, I run the risk of having to hide from crowds like an A-list celebrity. Um, hardly. But the warning is founded in a real fear. I told the critic I'd get some bigger sunglasses and take my chances. So far, my anonymity is safe.

THE CRITIC IS quick to find unpleasant consequences in any writing wish once fulfilled. What if you get a deal with your dream publisher? The critic will then warn you about possible nasty reviews. Or my personal favorite: what if you hate the cover? Yes, it would be sad to have a cover I didn't love, but this is by no means a reason to give up on publishing the book. And if this is a make-it-or-break-it point, it is possible to publish the book yourself to maintain full creative control of how it looks, including choosing the cover designer and final image.

We could go on and on with this, looking at authors who got giant advances and then were attacked by other writers who felt the amount was unfair. There are always unexpected outcomes to wishes coming true. Yes, if you got a million-dollar advance, you'd most likely be in a different tax bracket, but is this possibility a reason to give up on writing the book at all? Especially as that advance would enable you to hire someone to help you manage it responsibly, right?

I FIND it incredibly useful to make a list of all the terrible things my critic thinks will happen if my big wishes come true. Think about what you want most of all from writing your book. Write every dream you've got on this list. Go big — if you want a movie deal with your favorite actor playing your lead character, write that down. Review the list. Is there anything else? Make sure you listen up for the quiet wishes hiding in the back of your mind. Those deserve to be part of this, too.

ONCE YOU'RE sure you've got everything, re-read the list, picturing as vividly as you can what it would feel like if each of these wishes came true. Close your eyes and envision accepting the award, seeing your book in your favorite bookshop, walking onto the studio lot to watch the cast filming scenes you wrote. Feel it as if it's real.

Then let the critic go wild in response. Take a page per wish and explore the side effects the critic is most afraid will happen if these wishes come true. I like to write "if this happens, then..." at the top of the page and see what comes out. The critic can really come up with some extreme consequences. It will feel melodramatic. If the critic is telling you that you'll end up deathly ill and have no friends left the moment you get that dream publishing deal, write that down. You don't have to accept these fears, just acknowledge them.

DON'T WORK through every fear in one session. Take this process in stages. Your nervous system struggles to determine what's real and what's just in your imagination, so don't flood it. Journal these responses over a few days or a week, taking even longer depending on how many scenarios your critic generates. After you write about the critic's concerns, make sure you fully disengage from each one. Shake your hands and if it's available to you, find a way to shake your entire body. Taking a shower or bath can help, too.

Once you've gone through all the wishes and let the critic share its fears, let that writing sit for at least a day before you come back to it. Read through with a detached mindset.

Ask yourself if each fear is a problem. Some of them will shrivel up as you read them a second time. They may feel ridiculous enough to give you a good laugh. Some will still feel charged, though, and it's important to take those seriously. If you hit on a fear that really feels awful, ask yourself how you would handle it if that came to pass. How would you manage this distressing outcome?

It's ok if these side effects feel extremely unlikely. You don't need to agree with the critic about whether these concerns are hiding in the shadows at every turn. This is simply a chance to ask if you believe you could get through whatever life threw at you in response to finishing this book.

If you couldn't, what are ideas — other than not writing the book — that would help avoid this outcome? Often, having a rough plan in place is enough for the critic to back off and let you keep working.

The critic thrives in vague spaces of undefined dread. By taking time to hear out what its fears are and preparing a possible plan if they occurred, the critic's power over your choices diminishes. You decide what problems are too big for you to manage and worth adjusting your plan for, and which ones would merely be a brief annoyance that would soon be forgotten.

QUESTIONS TO PONDER:

- What is your wildest hope for your book?
- What would huge success look like for you?
- What is so audacious a dream you can barely even admit it to yourself?
- What negative outcome is truly unacceptable to you?
- Is there any vague dread hovering around the idea of publishing your book? What details can you add to make this more concrete, so it's possible to address it more directly?

11

TEN OF CUPS

IN EACH OF the suits (Cups, Wands, Swords, and Pentacles/Coins) the Ten is the most intense concentration of that energy. With the Cups, it looks like big feelings. When pulled in a traditional reading, the Ten of Cups usually represents "happily ever after."

However, as with the Nine of Cups we just explored, happily ever after is a loaded concept for writers. It spans multiple levels, so let's peel them away to the depths underneath.

ON THE SURFACE, reaching happily ever after for a project is a wonderful thing. Let's call this the THE END moment we all long for. This point appears many times as you write a book. First, getting to the end of the first draft is a huge success. We've accomplished our dream! But wait until someone tries to congratulate you on finishing writing your book.

"Oh no, it's just a draft," you say. "There's still a long way to go."

FAST FORWARD TO finishing the revision. "No, it's not actually finished," you protest to the well-wisher asking if it's celebration time yet. "I still need to get it published."

You can make an argument that you haven't yet reached the happy ending of this project until the end of time. If you want an agent and get one, then happily ever after is on hold until you get a book deal. If you get a book deal, you have to wait until you see the cover. Even if you love the cover, you have to wait and see reviews. Then the reviews come, and you've moved on to bestseller lists and placement there. Then there's the chance of awards. And on and on and on.

Even if your book is published exactly as you want it to be and you sell tons of copies, then there is the fear that it will never happen again. The sense of not having arrived at a happy ending yet continues even as you start the next book, if you let it.

The deep fear we find with the Ten of Cups is that there is never anything you're allowed to call an ultimate win, because there's always something new to strive for. Every time I taught Dream to Draft, my novel-writing intensive, watching writers coming across the finish line reaching the end of the draft was always bittersweet to watch.

"You did it!" I cheered.

"That's it?" they asked. "I thought there would be...
more."

WHEN WE DON'T ALLOW ourselves to celebrate the
steps along the way, we'll never feel satisfied at the so-
called big moments in the process. From early on in life,
we're conditioned to celebrate later. Save the money
Grandma gave you for your birthday, don't spend it now.
You'll be able to take holidays once you retire, focus on
work now. Work now, play later. While this is an effective approach to saving money, it's not at all true for celebrating milestones in your writing.

The beginning of the 2020s have been a huge
reminder that saving all our enjoyment for later doesn't
lead to a satisfying life. And postponing our enjoyment of
our writing until we've done enough to "deserve" it
means we'll never believe we've done enough. That bar
rises higher and higher the more progress we make.

**How to celebrate your happy ending
sooner**

The exercise that gives us the most perspective about
how exciting the milestone we've just crossed is this question:

"HOW WOULD **the you of five years ago feel,
upon learning what you've just done?"**

Maybe we're no longer impressed with having
written a first draft of a novel, now that we know we can.
But before you started the draft, it seemed like an impos-

sible hill to climb. The most heartbreaking thing I witness as a writing coach and teacher is my clients and students achieving things they never believed they could, only for the critic to immediately try to convince them that their success wasn't so impressive after all.

But do you know who is always impressed? The you of five years ago. That you would be gobsmacked to know that you've finished the first chapter, or sent out a pitch to an agent, or revised part two, or whatever you've reached THE END on. Former you was nowhere near as experienced a writer as you are now, and would be dancing in the street if they thought it was possible to do what you've just done.

This question protects you from getting jaded about your wins throughout writing your book. If we don't learn to celebrate the happy ending points because they turn to dust as soon as we reach them, then we lose the joy in our writing over time. We fear that what we're doing doesn't matter to anyone, and that there isn't any point. I assure you: there is a point, but we have to practice seeing the satisfaction in writing all along the way to feel it.

DON'T WAIT FOR AN "IMPORTANT" day when you think you're supposed to celebrate to raise a toast to your efforts. This will feel a bit silly at first. Do it anyway. The critic will tell you that you haven't done anything significant, but books are written in small steps over long periods, and we need to train ourselves to celebrate the small wins in order to be able to enjoy the big ones when they arrive.

AS WE'VE COME through the Cups, all the fears in that suit have led us to this moment. We've worried about how connected we are to the idea, how much we love it, how much others will love it, if it will end up being a huge disappointment, or if we'll only see the parts that aren't working, if we'll involve our own memories and experience and cause troubles, get distracted and pulled all over the place, want to leave the whole thing behind, have all our wishes come true, or never reach a point that feels like the end.

These are the fears that pull on our emotions. They hit us in the gut and feel the most wrenching. Don't worry if you don't recognize all of them. No need to fear not being afraid! Everyone has a different fingerprint of fears that challenge them, based on their own experience and psychology.

We're moving on from the Cups now, into the world of the Wands. These fears are less rooted in emotion and more focused on drive, ambition, and motivation. Let's move into a new suit and transform a new cycle of fear together.

12

WANDS OVERVIEW

THE WANDS ARE OUR DRIVE, our energy, our force. A funny story, to encapsulate the feeling of the Wands:

When we first moved to Berlin, we had a temporary furnished flat while we secured work visas, I did a training course, and we each got jobs, so it was only after about eight months that we got a proper lease on a flat with our names on the doorbell. I was so excited to set things up the way I wanted and to have a room I could write in, rather than a corner of a tiny living room.

After we moved in, I discovered something disturbing. The outlets in the room designated as the office didn't work. My German wasn't perfect, but it was good enough to speak on the phone, so I called the landlord and complained.

"We've just moved in, and the small room has no power. The outlets do not function properly — they do not provide power. I need to work and I cannot. Please repair this right away!"

Germany is not known for leaping into action on bureaucratic matters, so I had to keep calling daily until finally, on about day 10, an electrician called me back.

I was delighted and leaped into my now much-rehearsed speech.

"I am so glad you have called because I have this enormous problem. There is no power in our working room. I cannot work without power!"

"Woah, woah, woah," he broke in. "I think you mean there is no electricity. This is not Star Wars."

I was a bit stunned by this speech until I realized my mistake. I had looked "power" up in the dictionary, not "electricity." So every day, I had been calling and yelling about not having the FORCE in my apartment. Every single day, for ten days.

However, even though that German electrician was able to get the electricity flowing into my workroom, there is no way he could have provided the FORCE.

That's where the Wands come in. The drive, desire and motivation to write, this is the force. Our relationship to this experience is complex, and gives rise to its own set of fears. We'll explore these from Ace to Ten, just as we did with the Cups, and hopefully by the end of the section, you'll never fear being without the force again.

13

ACE OF WANDS

A BURST OF ENERGY, a kick. Horses running out of the gate as the race begins. The starting gun: this is the energy of the Ace of Wands. Motivation swirls around you and you feel the impulse to start writing the book.

While the first spark of excitement feels exciting, it's also a point of vulnerability. Just as a small fire can get blown out by a strong gust of wind, so too can your excitement. Even as you charge toward the page, fear swirls around you.

"Can I actually do this?" This is the first question that trips writers up. The enormity of writing a book tends to hit you once you start, recognizing that you have no idea how the whole process will unfold. Objections crop up about having enough time, wondering if you have to start getting up at 5am to write this book. Will you have to spend all of your life force on this one uncertain project?

. . .

FEAR that we don't have what it takes to get to the end of the book plagues nearly every writer early on in their writing life. I was no exception. When we are little, we constantly achieve things we've never done before. We learn to read and write, do math, speak at least one language, among countless other skills.

But these milestones are rarer as we age and we focus on honing existing skills rather than learning new ones. Suddenly "But I've never done this before!" becomes a reason not to do something, even though looking closer at this argument quickly shows how false it is.

If you're feeling overwhelmed by the bigness of writing an entire book, remember that it's not necessary — or even possible — to sit down and write the book cover to cover. When reading something we love, we can pick up a book in a comfy chair or on a long flight and go straight through, marveling at how seamless it feels.

We know in our minds that no one writes books cover to cover without stopping, but somehow we forget this when it's time to write our own. You don't need to have all the energy it takes to write the entire book today. It took me five years to write my first complete novel, and it takes months for me to write a complete nonfiction book. If all the energy that took appeared at once, I might explode.

The only energy you need right now is for the effort it will take you to write today. Tomorrow is a new beginning. Books are written in small steps, even though this isn't as satisfying a fantasy. Even if you like to write for hours at a time, you do that within the confines of a day, then set the work aside and return again after that day ends.

JACQUELINE WINSPEAR, author of the Maisie Dobbs series as well as other novels and a memoir, has been a guest on the Secret Library Podcast and the Oh! Murder Podcast. She shared a story that's become a favorite among my students and the members of the MYM Writing Lab community I run.

Whenever she feels overwhelmed with how much work she has to finish a book, she remembers a tip her husband shared: "Just do the next indicated thing."

You don't need to write 300 pages today, or even this month. Just turn up and do the next indicated thing. When we feel fear about getting to the end of the book, we are often zooming too far out on the process. The critic loves to make the picture too big for you to manage. The thing to remember is that everyone is just doing the next indicated thing, over and over, until they reach the end.

We run into the most trouble on our to-do lists. Most of us write down items that are impossible to complete in one setting or that have no clear goal. These look like "edit novel" or "work on book." This is a trap, as you have no idea when you've completed the task. If you find yourself writing items like this on your daily lists, you're setting yourself up to fail. It's necessary to break these items into actions you can complete in one sitting.

· · ·

TO USE OUR EXAMPLES ABOVE, "edit novel" becomes "re-read chapter 1 and make notes on potential changes." "Work on book" becomes "Make a list of essential scenes for Part 2." If you can't tell if you've finished a to-do list item, then it's not specific enough. We want you to have the satisfaction of completion and crossing it off.

The best to-do list items are almost always the next indicated thing. How do you know what the next indicated thing is? Let's look at a few more:

· WRITE a list of challenges the character needs to face in the story.

· Make a list of questions you haven't answered yet. Pick one and journal on possibilities.

· Gather up articles or books you want to read for research.

· Set a timer for a non-scary amount of time and write part of a scene from your list.

· Email the friend who's an expert in an area that appears in your book and ask for a chat on the topic.

EACH OF THESE can be done in thirty minutes or less, moving the process forward. I've seen books written this way more than once. All you have to do today is show up and do the next indicated thing.

WHENEVER YOU FEEL fear that you haven't got what it takes to write this book, ask yourself if you have what it takes to spend fifteen minutes with your book today. Keep asking that question over and over and showing up to the process.

When you don't have the time or energy for fifteen minutes, try five. And if five is too much, then rest. We all hit walls along the way with writing, and sometimes rest is the best answer. Force and drive aren't the only components of writing, so if you need to shift over to reading and mulling the ideas of the book over rather than pressing forward, know that's valid, too.

By sticking to manageable steps forward that you trust your ability to finish, you'll increase your confidence — and your motivation — to continue. By setting concrete goals and marking off each time you complete one, you'll see that you can be trusted and that you absolutely have the ability to get through the book, and other books as well, if you want to. Just like we need to break down our task lists, we also need to break down the energy we imagine needing to write the whole project. You don't need to have all the energy today — it would be wasted if you did. Far more important to have the focus to take consistent steps forward and have the energy for that day's task. When you keep working that way, you'll get through the project with less grinding effort and more ease than you imagined. Just focus on today's work and be proud when you get it done.

QUESTIONS TO PONDER:

- What do jolts of inspiration feel like to you?

- How do you feel about learning new things?
- Do you prefer beginning new projects or finishing them?
- What comes up for you when starting a big project?
- Do you like breaking down big tasks into little steps or do you prefer to dive in right away?
- What feels scary about beginnings?

14

TWO OF WANDS

ARE YOU A PLOTTER OR A PANTSER? This question comes up any time writers discuss process. For many people, the thought of planning out a book in advance is terrifying. While I have seen those who lay out the entire book in a jam-packed spreadsheet or treatment before they get down to the task of drafting, other writers fear that deciding what happens in advance will kill all the joy that comes from flying by the seat of their pants.

I am not here to convince anyone that planning is better than discovery writing. However, making a choice not to try something for yourself at all because it seems scary does you and your writing a disservice. There isn't one type of planning, just as all writers approach pantsing differently.

The first question to ask yourself is what about the planning feels undesirable. Do you hate the idea of spreadsheets, whereas index cards feel more fun? Or does having any kind of agenda for the story beforehand feel like it kills all your enjoyment?

ONE METHOD TO clarify how much planning would be helpful is to think about how you like to travel. Do you prefer to depart having each day laid out from morning till night? Do you want not only hotel and travel reservations, but all your meals chosen and reserved in advance, too? Or do you prefer to show up at the train station, have a look at the board and choose a destination without anything sorted ahead of time?

There is a whole spectrum of options in between, of course, but if you like a guided tour that covers every must-have experience at a destination, it's likely you'll be riddled with anxiety writing a novel without having a list of essential scenes to check off as you go. If the thought of committing to restaurants and activities before you depart makes you feel claustrophobic, then perhaps you'd be happier free-writing on your story in general and digging into the characters and how they might react in a variety of situations, which may or may not appear in the book. Or having the content of scenes planned but making the locations spontaneous might create a balance with more ease.

Above all, know that plans can — and do — change. Even if you have a detailed outline you've pored over, there is a chance that something won't feel write once you start writing. That's ok. No need to adhere senselessly to a plan you're no longer satisfied with. And from the other side, if you spend the equivalent of a day on holiday with no plans and end up feeling frustrated and overwhelmed, it's also ok to pause and make a rough plan before continuing.

THE ENTIRE PURPOSE of making a plan is to clarify the story and to make writing it feel more satisfying. As you work through the book, watch what feels easy and what feels challenging. If you haven't written a book before, you'll be learning how you like to write books at the same time you're learning how you want to write this specific book. That's a big chunk of learning, but it's also quite exciting. Remember that you're learning: you don't have to do this perfectly. Mistakes and wrong turns provide even more knowledge than getting it right imme-diately.

It's easy to get sucked into advice that promises to give you the perfect plan, usually to finish your book quickly. I see loads of guides out there promising to help you write huge numbers of words in very short periods of time. If that's something you're on fire to do, then some of that advice may be useful. However, in my experience, every plan needs to be tailored to you and the way you write.

IF PART of your fear of planning is the fear that if you follow your own instincts, you'll get it wrong, we need to take a short pause here.

Let's define what "getting it wrong" means, because the critic loves to take control of this concept early on. It may argue that if a book takes you more than a certain amount of time to write, if you are uncertain about sections of the story or character motivation or anything else about the book, you are in danger of getting it wrong. This is just not true. All this uncertainty is part of being a writer. No plan can prevent you from having doubts along the way. If you plan and still have doubts, that's normal. And if you don't plan because you're afraid it will take away the thrill of the unknown, remember that no plan can obliterate that completely. It's just a question of just how much uncertainty you like to have.

This may change over time. When I first started recording interviews for the Secret Library Podcast, I made a lot of notes in preparation. I read the author's book, if that was what we were discussing and came up with a list of questions I thought would make an interesting episode. But at some point during the nearly nine years I've had the show, that changed. I still read the book, but the list of prepared questions fell away. At first, I made one or two, and now I make none. I learned that the questions I prepped in advance were just my best take on what I'd like to talk about with this writer. But as soon as I met them and we began the conversation, that changed. They almost always said something I got excited about and wanted to dive deeper into. The interviews I was happiest with followed this thread, and I never came back to the prepared list structuring the show.

· · ·

IT'S the same with a plan for a book. You lay out the best take you can beforehand to get writing, knowing it may change once you start the actual process of writing the material. Perhaps I have my best take in an outline of what I think my characters will do. But once I start writing scenes, I see them in action and hear them speak. At this point, I may have entirely new ideas about what the heart of the story is. That's ok. I can either reformulate my plan, if that feels helpful, or I can keep going flying without a net and see where it takes me.

Neither of these methods is superior, but one may be a better fit for you than the other. Try everything that you're curious about, let go of what doesn't work, and customize all the approaches you take. Eventually, you'll have a plan that suits you, just like something that was tailor made to get you through the story, hopefully without feeling scared you're doing it wrong. Going astray is part of the process. Embrace it, learn from it, and keep coming back.

The best plan you can use is the one that works for you. Take notes on the aspects that are helpful, forget the things that aren't, and your efforts will pay off in the form of a book before you know it.

QUESTIONS TO PONDER:

- Do you identify more as a "plotter" or a "pantster"?

- How do you feel about planning writing projects?
- What is your perfect day while traveling?
- How does your favorite travel approach relate to your preferred method of writing?
- What makes you feel most prepared to write?

15

THREE OF WANDS

NO MATTER how happy you are with your plan, eventually you have to step past it and begin writing, otherwise the book will never exist. This is the realm of the Three of Wands: the fear of acting on your plan.

You'll recognize this fear as a force field that forms around the book itself. You can make notes, scratch ideas into a notebook, but once you turn to writing THE BOOK, that feels like too much. The Two and Three of Wands work together as a pair of delusions. You worry about making the perfect plan with the Two and once you get to the Three where it's time to act on the plan and write, any wobbling creates temptation to go back to the Two and refine the plan.

As we've discussed, there is no perfect outline, so you can't plan your way out of fear around starting the manuscript. The fear of beginning to write is actually a complex web all tangled together.

If you are scared that you are incapable of writing

well enough to execute your plan — as if this were an entrance exam — if you are afraid you've actually got nothing to say, if the blinking cursor feels like an accusation that you just aren't ready for this, you're in the grip of the Three of Wands.

THE FEAR of the blank page at the beginning of a project is one of the most familiar, as films love to show. It's easy to dramatize, and most people can relate to staring into the abyss, where all ideas, no matter how exciting they seemed at first, crumble away. First drafts take the most energy, in my experience, because you are exerting the effort required to go from nothing to something. In later drafts, you get to shape and reshape the existing text, but starting with nothing brings up far more doubt.

In order to confront this fear, it's necessary to lower the pedestal. We are all guilty of placing ideas high up in an exalted position, hoping our writing can reach the level we dream of. But as long as your idea is far up in the stars and you are on the ground, you're never going to be able to work together effectively.

ANNE LAMOTT HAS LONG BEEN a champion of the shitty first draft approach, taking all the pressure off THE BOOK off by embracing the fact that the first time through will look nothing like the glorious creation you'd hoped for. This is sound advice.

I have a student who likes to write "This doesn't

count" at the top of notebook pages when working on the early stages of a draft. It's true: it doesn't count until you've decided it does.

The issue you're fighting isn't whether you have a good enough plan. What you're actually coming up against is training we received in our education, messages that are thankfully now shifting. Given that much of our education system is designed to be an efficient way of measuring and sorting innate abilities, most of us were quickly funneled into the paths of study we showed the most aptitude for right away. But this discounts that fact that many skills can be learned, and that — given the opportunity — many people would choose to learn them.

After spending our formative years taking tests or getting assessed as "good at math" or "strong in language" or science or art or history, we were encouraged toward some areas of story and away from others. Add in the fact that some careers earn a higher salary or status than others in our families and society and you've got an anvil of pressure sitting on you.

EVEN IF YOU showed skill in writing and were encouraged in that direction, this is still inside of a system that believed some people just knew how to do this and some didn't. We had to prove we were the writers, not that we enjoyed writing and wanted to learn more about it.

With all this baggage hanging around your neck, it's no wonder that every time you begin a new project, it feels like another exam where you have to show excellent results quickly and with very little effort in order to justify your right to continue.

I can think of hardly any other skill out there that we do so frequently while fearing we are actually terrible at it. In today's world, we write all day long. Phone calls have given way to emails and texts. We communicate in writing constantly, and yet we think we're unable to articulate our thoughts at all.

Could most of us learn to write more effectively with practice? The ability to learn isn't the issue, though. What we fear most is that we've already failed and there's no way to change this.

If you are under pressure to validate your ability to write from the very first draft, why wouldn't you freeze up when beginning? Why wouldn't making just a few more notes seem more reasonable than diving into the manuscript itself?

TO NAVIGATE THIS FEAR, I find turning to another art form for comparison, that of painting, helps enormously. Specifically painting that aims to portray a recognizable subject, like a landscape or a portrait. If you've ever had the chance to look at painters' sketches, you'll see that they don't dive into the painting without exploring possibilities in advance. They make drawings to consider composition and placement, much like we as writers make notes about ideas and character. But the point when painting has a leg up on writing is when we turn to THE CANVAS.

When restorers make scans of paintings, they confirm

that masterpieces we find in museums don't begin with a blank canvas. The artist doesn't step up and paint the whole thing blind. They sketch on the canvas itself and build the painting from there. Even oil paint shifts and areas get painted out and changed before the image is complete.

AS YOU BEGIN the manuscript and fear of the blank page appears, know that it's ok to write in a sketch form and build. The blank page can feel like it has a force field around it, preventing you from starting. The best way to break through is to make a mark, even an imperfect one. Get one crappy sentence down and then see what happens from there. You don't need to prove your right to write this book by writing a perfect draft from the first pass. Not even skilled authors with multiple books published write this way. Allow yourself the shitty first draft. Create the something you can build from, and enjoy the rebellion that comes from writing without anyone giving you permission. The only permission you need to begin is your own.

QUESTIONS TO PONDER:

- What holds you back when you begin writing the actual manuscript?
- How do you feel unprepared to write?

- What permission or assurance do you need to begin?
- Who are you hoping will grant you this permission?
- How would it feel to start because you decided you were ready?

16

FOUR OF WANDS

ONCE YOU BREAK the force field and begin writing in earnest, the fears transform. Putting words on the page is no longer the issue, so the critic changes tactics and attacks anew. This is when the question of "is it good?" usually shows up.

Good as an adjective for writing is one most writers strive for, but the longer you write the more you'll realize what a useless description it is. "Good" is one hundred percent subjective and there is no good writing that rules them all. No one's book is beloved by every reader throughout time.

As you write, the critic will produce roadblocks, and there is no more thorny question than that about a book's goodness. The fear that comes with the Four of Wands goes even further than that. What if you wrote a book thinking it was good, celebrating how well the writing was going, the critic suggests, only to realize you were celebrating writing that was actually terrible?

. . .

WHAT IF YOU have been working hard, writing the actual book and feeling satisfied, not knowing that the book is actually an unsalvageable heap of trash? This is the question the critic whispers in your ear, along with the suggestion that you have no idea what you're doing, while you attempt to return to the page day after day to take the steps required to finish the thing.

Cynics are suspicious of celebration. They sniff derisively at enthusiasm, never dance with abandon, and judge those who do. If you get too excited or start thinking that perhaps you're really onto something, the critic worries you're going to get very badly hurt. Better to think the book isn't good and give up, then to finish it thinking it's great, only to be rejected later.

What the critic doesn't accept is that celebrating the process is how books get written. It champions being realistic, when really it is operating as a killjoy that stops the entire engine from firing. Beyond this is a secret the critic absolutely doesn't want you to know: that it's very difficult, let alone impossible, to assess how well the writing has gone right after you complete it.

AUTHOR CORY DOCTOROW came on the Secret Library Podcast and spoke to just this point. He has a writing routine of 500 words a day when working on a book. Some days it goes well, and some days it feels awful. He maintains that, when he goes back in to revise, he can never tell the difference between the two. Having published many books, translated into multiple languages, it's clear he doesn't need to. How we feel about what we've written, and the quality of the writing are two entirely different things. Don't try to write and judge your writing in the same session — this has the same effect as trying to hold down the accelerator and the brake at the same time when driving. You get nowhere while wasting huge amounts of energy in the process.

This fear twists your motivation by forcing you to focus on things that do matter, but not in a way that's helpful. Given that you'll spend many hours and weeks and months, possibly even years, working on any book you write, enjoying the process is a priority. But this isn't because it's an accurate metric of the value of the writing. You deserve to enjoy writing the book because your experience as a writer counts. However, the feeling that the heavens have opened and the celestial light has poured down on you has absolutely no bearing on how successful the writing was that day.

WE CAN SUM the fear of the Four of Cups up as the fear of celebrating at the wrong point, or for the wrong reason. I am, as my students and clients well know, a huge fan of celebration. But the celebration I advocate is about the process, not the result. Celebrate the fact that you showed up to write today, no matter how long you worked. Celebrate that you made notes on an idea, that you stuck with it. Don't make judgments about the result. If we're only allowed to celebrate the outcome of our work, the road ahead will be lonely and painful indeed.

Once you complete your book, depending on your goals for publishing, much of the next steps are out of your control. Traditional publishing, at least in the U.S. and U.K. markets, is contingent on winning over an agent and then a publishing house. I bring this up not to discourage, but to point out that celebrating the steps you have control over is how you can get to a finished book in the first place.

INSTEAD OF LETTING fear decide the criteria for celebration, we can get ahead of the issue by setting our own. Choose what's worthy of celebration for you and make it easy to attain. The critic will hate this. It will fight you, call you silly, and warn you that this will lead to your ruin. It won't. In fact, this is the most likely change that will lead to results.

I created a whole course on this topic, Mini Wins, which clarifies a system of breaking whatever project you want to complete down into steps so small you can complete them even on a shitty day. A student, who took the course and then joined the MYM Lab, my annual writing community, said with some shock, "It turns out it actually really works."

Celebration is powerful, so turn it toward the moments you show up, even though it's challenging, even though you're afraid what you're writing isn't any good at all. You need to have words to form into the final book, so celebrate yourself for every point you choose to add more to the page. That is worthy of a dance party.

. . .

BECAUSE THE MORE YOU set goals you can achieve easily, and show yourself that you can meet them, the more you begin to believe. The only obstacle to Neo becoming The One was believing in himself, to use the classic example. But this is the biggest barrier to becoming an author: accepting that you can be one. And behaving like an author is the best way to reach that point: showing up, writing, and celebrating that you've written, even if your easy first step is five minutes a day. I've seen more than writer smash a block and figure out the thorniest of plot tangles in a daily session of that amount of time. It works.

Once you've decided when and why you celebrate, you actually have to do it. Decide not only what you will celebrate, but how. If you said you'd have a dance party every time you do a five-minute writing session, once the timer goes off, that music had better come on. Because the second you start letting the critic tell you those five minutes don't count and you move the goal posts, you lose the chance to acknowledge yourself completing that step. Celebrating hitting the mark over time is the best way to see the big picture: that getting a book done is just a series of manageable goals you set and achieved.

If you let the critic increase your goal out of fear rather than excitement, you'll risk your overall success, too. Decide what enough looks like in advance, and never reassess that when you're sitting at your desk working. Do what you set out to do, and celebrate yourself each time. This is how books are made.

. . .

QUESTIONS TO PONDER:

- What landmarks have you reached in your writing process?
- Were you excited to reach them?
- Did you celebrate them, or feel you simply had to press on?
- How would it feel to celebrate the things you achieved in small steps?
- What can you celebrate today?

17

FIVE OF WANDS

WRITING REQUIRES TAKING A STAND. As storytellers, we have to make choices. We can't follow every possibility to every potential ending, or else we'd be writing forever. We also can't write essays that explore every side of an argument or a concept. We have to choose, and choosing means someone will disagree with us.

It's tempting to try to please everyone, but this doesn't solve the issue. If we don't follow a clear path, then everyone gets lost.

Through the Wands, we've looked at what we are impassioned about and what we are driven to share. Following this path ensures that those who are similarly driven will connect with your work. However, it also means that some people won't.

The critic clobbers you. "They're going to hate it. You can't write this." It claims that someone hating your work is a reason not to share it. But what if someone hating your work wasn't a good judge of its value?

. . .

IN THE UNITED STATES, a huge number of books are currently banned. Many parents don't want their children to have access to stories about LGBTQIA+ youth. Authors are watching their work getting pulled from shelves, even books that previously won awards. Are these books no longer valuable if some people want them banned?

Even on a less dramatic scale, I've often found myself at a loss when reading a book many people have loved but just doesn't click for me. Even if I don't love a book, many other readers may feel differently. I've also loved books so much I was pushing them on every person I spoke to after finishing them. Not everyone agrees with my opinion.

We need to separate the two statements the critic throws out together: "They're going to hate it" and "You can't write this." These two ideas aren't fused together. Given the incredible variety of human minds and life experience and preferences this world contains, it is impossible that everyone will love your book. But this doesn't mean you can't — or shouldn't — write it.

Imagine every book in the world that someone disliked suddenly disappearing. The shelves in libraries and bookstores would be empty. What if those writers let this fear shut them down?

LET'S look at this from another angle. Often the books people love the most are those that inspire the most controversy. Books that take a stand or tell a story in a new way inspire both love and rejection by readers. I've had the concept of a book turn me off completely, only to find out it's a friend's new favorite.

What if some people hating your book was the side effect of writing something groundbreaking? Why is it so hard for us to hold both sides of this experience? I believe it's because of how we're taught literature early on.

In many areas, we label some portion of creative output as classics. This exists in music, writing, dance, art, poetry, theater, film and pretty much any creative field you can imagine. In school, we read the classics. By learning that there are universally acclaimed books, we absorbed the idea that this was successful writing.

But these books aren't universally beloved. I, personally, loved *Jane Eyre* but my husband and step-daughter both hated it. Do we need to travel back in time and tell Charlotte Brontë that her book is doomed and she shouldn't finish it?

WHAT THE FIVE of Wands asks of us is to embrace inspiring strong emotion. If we fear people disliking our book, there is no room for other people to love it either. Writing something bold is a risk. And it can feel terrifying to commit to that risk, but the price of inspiring passion in readers is that it isn't always the passion we wanted.

What if our goal wasn't to fear negative opinions? What if we welcomed them? The fear of people disliking our work stems from our fear of being too much. As writers, we explore emotion deeply. We look at characters pushed to the end of their tolerance in devastating situations. We take on topics that matter to us. If I only inspired a tepid response with my story, that would feel like the true failure.

But the inner critic's goal is, as always, to keep you safe. Its impulses come from society's instincts for us to be good little people and not make a fuss. But is that what we really want with our writing? Do we just want to neatly preserve the status quo?

When we speak up about topics that matter to us, be that social justice, the environment, society's choices, or even the dynamics that exist between people, these aren't small neutral things. How would it feel to shift your goal to inspiring emotion in your reader, whatever that emotion looked like?

If we accept this fear as part of the process, can that become yet another way fear shows us that we're on to something? If the critic says "They're going to hate this," can we pause and ask these questions instead of running away?

- Who is going to hate it? Can I clarify who "they" is?
- Do I care about their opinion?
- Who will love this work? What reader can I picture cheering for my book?
- Which reader matters more to me?
- Am I willing to tolerate one "they" hating my work if other readers love it?

- Is this story one I care enough about to fight for?

TEASING APART the critic's announcements can turn this fear around quickly. Because if we find a reader we care about writing for, the one who might hate our work doesn't matter nearly as much.

Who you're willing to fight for, from characters to readers, can protect you from this fear nearly instantly.

Keep asking the critic "who will hate it?" and keep going.

18

SIX OF WANDS

EVERY WEEK, *Publisher's Weekly* posts a summary of books acquired by editors at various publishing houses. The authors' names and awards parade by, open to public scrutiny. While most authors dream of this moment, it's also a point when fear strikes.

Not only do we feel fear when we imagine being left on the side of the road as the parade of published authors passes by, we can also freeze up when imagining we're marching ourselves, representing success. This is a vulnerable moment. You've worked for years on a story that was all yours and suddenly it's broadcast to the world.

Being publicly acknowledged as a writer with a book deal triggers impostor syndrome. Even if you've gotten an agent and a book deal, this is rarely enough for the critic. Rather than feeling a sense of accomplishment, public success can feel like a set-up that leads to even more people being disappointed. Whereas before it was just you with hopes for the book, now, as a "writer with a book deal," its failure would hurt an agent, an editor, and everyone working on the project as well.

ANY FEAR we have of calling ourselves writers moves into high gear at this point. The ability to back away from writing without anyone noticing is gone now that your book has been announced. This doesn't just happen with traditional publishing either: announcing a forthcoming book you put out independently can feel just as scary.

Whether someone else is announcing it on our behalf or we're telling the world, "I've written this book and you'll be able to read it soon," can feel like a target is suddenly on your back. The story of The Emperor's New Clothes sums this fear up perfectly, but with a twist: we believe we're naked and are hoping that no one else notices.

"What if this is all a terrible mistake and everyone's going to hate my book and me?"

As long as we've simply been daydreaming about writing a book someday, this scenario was never a possibility. We could imagine what it would be like as a published author without reality getting in the way. But now that people know about the book, we could get hurt by the actual experience diverging too much from our dream.

The critic is kicking into high gear because it fears the world isn't safe for you now. The critic may tell you that you'll be a laughingstock at best and the recipient of death threats if this doesn't work out at worst.

. . .

EVEN IF YOU'RE far from the point where you pitch or publish your book, this fear can still spring up. Seeing someone else get a book deal can bring it to the surface, as can feeling that you're getting close to finishing. The critic jumps ahead to the next unknown point in the process to dump a bucket of ice-cold fear down the back of your neck.

SHOULD you feel anxiety about a big public reaction to your work, take that concern seriously and reflect on how it feels safest to share that writing. When Alexandra Franzen had a vivid dream, she couldn't get the story out of her mind. She dreamt that a new technology allowed her, just after her death, to be brought back to life for twenty-four hours. Her dream self took risks and followed her heart, living a gorgeous day gifted to her by this miraculous invention before waking up.

Eventually, she wrote the dream as her first fiction project. She wrote nonfiction professionally, even consulting for others, but had never considered writing a novel before. What would happen if she announced that she was now a novelist, too? This felt far too scary.

Instead of publishing the book, Alexandra sent it as a gift to her email newsletter list, explaining she wasn't sure what it was, but she hoped they'd like it. The subscribers felt like a safe place to share this story. They turned out to be an enthusiastic audience, and told Alexandra how much they loved it. People asked if they could share it, as they knew friends would be just as inspired.

She added the book for sale on her website as a download, not yet ready to make it available to the general public. People kept reading the story. Finally, Alexandra felt ready to share it as a published book. Despite the terror gripping her, she wrote to a publisher she'd worked with before for her nonfiction, asking if they might know an agent or publisher who'd consider looking at the short novel she'd written.

Her contact replied that this was incredible timing and asked her to send it immediately. They'd just gotten out of a meeting discussing publishing fiction for the first time. Alexandra's book, *So This is the End: A Love Story*, ended up coming out through that publisher, Mango. I love this whole publication story, as it shows that taking the time to feel her way through the process meant the timing was just right when she reached out to publish.

WE USED to believe there was only one way to publish a book: get an agent, they get a book deal, and the book ends up on shelves. This was the publishing dream for writers in the U.S. and the U.K. The advent of indie publishing was seen as a sacrifice, a result that meant giving up on the traditional publishing dream. For many years, publicly identifying as an indie author meant you'd let go of believing traditional publishing was for you.

But now, the boundaries are fluid. How we send our work and our author identities out into the world can change depending on our vision for that book. Many writers publish themselves, but end up with traditional book deals later on. Other writers publish traditionally for years and then choose to put a project out on their own so they maintain full control.

YOU AREN'T COMMITTING to one identity or one reality as a writer the moment you share what you're working on publicly, whether you talk about writing on social media, publish a piece or a whole book.

The fears that come up can help you clarify your needs when publishing or speaking publicly about writing.

Knowing your boundaries helps set up plans and structures to keep you feeling safe, even when your writing and your author self exist out in the world. Getting clear on these fears means you can make good choices that fit for you.

QUESTIONS TO PONDER:

- What scares me about people knowing I'm a writer?
- How would I feel if people read my work?
- What is the worst thing I can imagine happening if I'm publicly acknowledged as a writer?
- How do I feel about protecting my privacy?
- What boundaries do I want to hold with the outside world, even if I'm a successful writer?

19

SEVEN OF WANDS

AFTER HAVING A MEASURE OF SUCCESS, as we saw with the Six of Wands, we don't simply ride off into the sunset with our parade. Public recognition represents a point of arrival, and the Seven of Wands is what comes after.

I think of this card as everything that we associate with "second novel syndrome." You've reached a point of celebration and recognition, and now there is the need to create something new. Will it receive the same acclaim? Can you make this happen again?

In many decks, the image that accompanies this card is a figure standing on a hill with six wands extending into view, battling to knock the figure down with the seventh wand brandished as a weapon. Time to defend your position, but what position is that exactly?

This looks different for everyone, as always. Perhaps you've written a successful book but now want to try something different. Fear of being rejected for this choice paralyzes you. "Do I follow my curiosity? It worked out before. But now people love that book — do I have to keep writing that same type of book forever?"

Musicians face this fear, especially those who have songs and albums that people love and want to hear on tour. The Seven of Wands is the struggle to stay successful while playing something new when everyone just wants to hear the greatest hits.

PRIOR TO WRITING THIS BOOK, I thought of this card as the way fame can turn on you. If a writer is very successful and does get the book deal or huge sales or acclaim then people can strike them down out of jealousy, leaving the writer having to defend themselves against attack as a result of success.

As I dug into this card, however, I noticed something important: the figure is holding one wand, while the other six are attacking. What if this card represents the direct consequences of the parade? You may encounter fear of being visibly successful and shy away from that at face value with the Six, but once we reach the Seven, the parade has already happened.

The fears that come up here are the ones you experience once you've been acknowledged publicly. An award nomination, a piece published in a publication you've long hoped to break into; even earning over a certain amount of money from writing can trigger terror.

WHAT ARE you afraid you'll have to fight off once you succeed with writing? Nasty comments on review sites feel intimidating to many newly published authors. Even knowing that many more people will read your work now can feel scary, as it means you have well and truly lost control of what they think. At high levels of success, you may fear people treating you differently because you earn more money now than you did before.

However, these aren't all guaranteed, other than nasty comments on review sites. I won't lie about that one. But these comments say far more about the person posting them than the writer of the book. They shred your writing because they are scared to risk sharing their own. I've witnessed an upsurge of thoughtless comments on vulnerable posts on Substack recently, and almost always when I click through to see the commenter's account, they haven't shared a single post themselves. Far easier to criticize someone else than to open themselves up to someone speaking harshly about their own work.

Beyond nasty comments, we are absolutely not guaranteed fame, influxes of large sums of money, awards, or any recognition at all. These results are unclear, though, and the critic thrives on scaring you with the unknown. Once one stage of writing becomes familiar and feels manageable, the critic leaps to the next unknown point and brings fears to the surface.

While we begin afraid we could never write enough to fill a novel, even after we publish that novel, our critic is still looking ahead at the next unfamiliar step to scare us.

. . .

ONCE WE'VE HAD success it's usually one of the following themes that appears:

- Everyone will hate your book
- If they didn't hate this one, they'll hate the next one
- Getting optioned for a film? You'll hate the film
- If you don't hate the film, everyone else will
- You'll never have another good idea
- The previous success was a fluke

THE CRITIC CAN REMIX these fears on repeat forever, like a DJ sampling tropes of terror to make you dance. But here's the essential piece with the Seven of Wands: you can walk away from this battle. The first step is to clarify which hills are worth dying on, so to speak. Once you have more visibility and acclaim as a writer, you don't need to spend all your time on this hill, holding your ground. The process of not fighting against every fear is one of the rites of passage you'll experience once your work strikes a chord in the world.

Yes, it's important to defend your position by setting boundaries. For example, you may wish to remove your email address from your web page if you prefer not to have people contact you directly. This is an empowered defense.

However, you don't need to spend all your time (or any of your time) in the comments section of your site or a review page, debating with those leaving nasty comments to try to bring them around. If people don't understand what you hoped to communicate in your book, it's not going to be possible to clarify that en masse.

When fears come up about the aftermath of success, ask yourself "Is this something that's essential for me to fight?"

Not just "Do I want to fight this?" but "Is it essential?" What you'll need to defend and protect above all once your writing is in the public space is your time and attention. Many writers share how much they miss the experience of writing their first novel because the pressure hadn't showed up yet. Writing a novel organically, on the schedule that suits us best, is wonderful, and if you write a successful book you may not have the luxury of that schedule again.

WHETHER PUBLISHING TRADITIONALLY OR INDEPENDENTLY, after a novel comes out and people enjoy it, the clock ticks on with other new fans now waiting for more of your writing. We know this feeling as readers, finishing a book we really loved and immediately searching for what else the author has written. When it's pointed at us as writers, it can feel distracting at best and debilitating at worst.

This fear is real. I bring this up not to intensify it, but to slow you down so you can grapple with it in advance, when you can make choices to empower yourself. If you don't want to be under pressure to write on a much faster schedule, then negotiate for a contract that doesn't expect a new book more frequently than you can write it. If you publish independently, it's worth considering other income streams so that you aren't dependent on a rapid-release schedule to make ends meet if it causes panic and debilitating stress.

The fears that arise with the Seven of Wands serve as clues to what you want to avoid in your writing career. Write them down as they come up and ask each one in turn: "What would it take for me to prevent this from happening?"

We can't prevent every fear from coming to pass, but I encourage you to have options and to consider which situations would feel unacceptable in advance. This way, the critic won't drive you to quit writing at all to prevent these fears from coming to pass.

Your control over the process isn't gone once you publish: your reality just changes as it would at any cross-roads. The more informed we are ahead of time, the more confidently we can move forward. Let's continue on, where we'll get some jolts of energy before the end of this suit.

QUESTIONS TO PONDER:

· What's the next unknown step in your writing process?

· Do you have control over how it happens?

· What would feel like a successful outcome for your book?

· Do you have any worries about how that would change your life?

· Is there anything that you need to set boundaries on for now?

· What choices about your book do you want to stay in control of?

20

EIGHT OF WANDS

HAVE you ever read a book that transformed what you thought was possible for your own writing? Whenever I find an author who breaks rules that I didn't realize I was trying to follow, I become practically drunk on the freedom. I call these "You mean we're allowed to do that now?" books. They are rare and transformative bolts of lightning. I live to find them most of all.

Sometimes these aren't even books I love, but the craft is so surprising I am just as delighted by the possibilities that they represent. When I read *Then We Came to the End* by Joshua Ferris, the idea of writing an entire novel with a collective "we" narrator shifted my sense of what a narrator could look like. Reading books without any formatted dialogue, with the lines that characters speak aloud folded into the prose, like Sally Rooney does, shook me out of a rigid sense of what conversations in books were "supposed" to look like. In addition, reading books from decades ago, or even hundreds of years ago, can have the same effect. We are impacted by our reading, whether we realize it or not, and continually expanding what we think is possible through our reading choices functions as the equivalent of a balanced diet.

EARLY ON IN our writing lives, we may dream of writing like a particular author. We hold their style, sensibility, and technique as the pinnacle of what we hope to achieve in our own writing. Meanwhile, we desperately fear outright copying. Plagiarism not only steps over the line of being inspired by another writer, it stops us from writing our own story. Many writers live with such intense fear of accidental plagiarism that they don't read anything remotely similar to what they are trying to write the entire time they're working on it. I've even heard of writers who try to write without reading at all.

The Eight of Wands is the fear of depending on the bolt of lightning from other writers. The terror that we might steal from another author is enough to destroy a writer's ability to create. Because the truth is, nothing gets created in a vacuum. Joshua Ferris wasn't the first writer to use a collective narrator. This goes all the way back to Greek theater and the construct of the chorus. Sally Rooney wasn't the first to weave dialogue into prose. You see the same technique in *All the Pretty Horses* by Cormac McCarthy, who was in turn influenced by someone he read, most likely. These approaches aren't plagiarism. Ferris pulls the chorus from Greek Tragedy into a modern office facing layoffs. Sally Rooney takes dialogue woven into prose into complex narratives of close relationships in contemporary times, which feels as far away from McCarthy's historical western as we can get.

BUT THESE AREN'T the only sources of inspiration these writers draw upon. Problems appear when writers don't vary their sources. If, for example, you love Isabel Allende and her lush magical realism and you love it so much that you only read her books over and over, it is inevitable that you will begin to sound like Isabel Allende and tell stories with very similar plots and characters.

However, if you also read Science Fiction and other literature, and folk takes, and books from a variety of eras, finding elements in all of these that you love, being inspired becomes a feature of your writing, not a liability. Suddenly your work is a curation of techniques and elements you love, rather than derivative of only one voice.

AUSTIN KLEON WRITES about this in his short but transformative book, *Steal Like an Artist*, which is one of the best antidotes to this fear that I can suggest. Author voice is this process of gathering approaches to writing that you love and filtering it through your own mind to create something entirely new. The sad thing about fear of being impacted by other writers is that it prevents you from fully developing your own style.

Other art forms have a different approach to this phenomenon. Music, in particular, has gone through cycles of inspiration that bounce between artists to shift and expand what's possible. Films feature homages to other directors and films and have elevated this to nearly their own language. Painting and visual art take what one artist has done and either build on it or deconstruct it in a way a viewer can track when walking through a museum or flipping through art books that follow art through the ages. Sometimes we can even watch it in one artist's work, like Piet Mondrian. He began as a representational painter, but kept distilling down the forms into geometric shapes, likely influenced by the Cubists, but then distilling color to the primary shades and 90-degree angles and thick black lines. Part of the joy of art is being in conversation with other artists through our work. But writers often fear participating in this conversation, usually because we fear we have nothing to offer without the influence of other writers.

A FAVORITE CONCEPT I learned when getting my Master's in Psychology was the idea of role theory. You are not the same person with your children as you are with your friends. You are still different with your colleagues versus your partner or your parents versus strangers. The role theory of mental health says that the more flexible we are in our ability to show up as a role that suits the situation we're in, the healthier we are.

We may fear early on in our writing lives that we have only one identity as a writer, and it's one that doesn't live up to our aspirations. If we doubt our own writing ability, then we may try to be Isabel Allende instead, because we deem her writing better than our own. But she became the writer she is by embracing all the aspects of her writing self. Over a writing career, every writer stumbles, gets stuck, is delighted with what they've written, and is unsure what will come next. And throughout their careers, writers engage with other writers, by both reading and engaging with them directly.

THE ANTIDOTE to the fear of being derivative is to lean into the impact of other writers more. Trust your own curiosity. Even if you and your best friend read the same stack of books, looking for sparks of inspiration, when you came to the bottom of the stack you'd each have an entirely different list of elements to draw on. We infuse what we write with our own fingerprint.

I KNOW a writer who admitted to me that one of his novels was originally meant to be co-authored with another person. They are good friends and write similar genres and share a compatible worldview. Before beginning the book, they worked together on the idea and a complete outline. Soon after starting the writing, they realized the limitations of writing together. As my friend put it, you each have to do seventy-five percent of the work. They decided to go ahead and each write their own version independently. Both books sold and got published not long apart.

Not a single critic noticed the similarity. None of their readers, neither editor. Nobody. If you expand your sources of inspiration and trust that you are drawn to the aspects of writing that are unique to you, your books will become reflections of the worldview that is yours alone. But you can't find this voice without participating in the world around you.

Read, react, and dream. Follow the thread of what lights you up. There, your stories truly come to life.

QUESTIONS TO PONDER:

- Which writers do you admire?
- Which books do you wish you had written?
- What innovations in style or writing delight you?
- What do you dislike in books you read?
- What's a genre you never read?
- How would it feel to read something entirely different, just to learn from it?

21

NINE OF WANDS

GETTING to the end is tiring. When you get close to finishing a book for the first time, you know for certain that books aren't written in a single bound. They're written by resisting the urge to run away over and over, coming back when it would be easier not to until they're finished. And right before the end, you can get very tired indeed.

The Nine of Wands is that point when you're past tired, but you can see the end not far ahead. It is the last push. The fear that hits us at this stage is that we'll collapse before we cross the finish line.

WHEN WE MOVED TO BERLIN, we spent the first nine months in a tiny furnished flat, less than one quarter the size of our home in LA. When we finally got our own long-term place, where we still live now, it came with a challenging feature: it's a fourth-floor walkup. For my readers in the U.S., this is a fifth-floor walkup for you, as the ground floor is counted as zero, and the numbers start after you've already climbed a flight of stairs. Living at the top of ten sets of stairs — two per level — reduces nearly everyone who comes to our home into a wheezing heap. We've gotten used to it, and most days it's tolerable, but occasionally I realize I'm sticking my keys into our downstairs neighbors' door, willfully blind to the fact that I've got another two sets of stairs to climb.

THIS IS the point when the Nine of Wands fear kicks in. It's the energy you need when you want to lie down and groan. You've expended your energy and motivation on this project until you're exhausted, yet there's still more to do. How is this possible?

As an irregular and untalented runner, I enjoy reading other people's stories about the sport. Murakami's book *What I Talk About When I Talk About Running* is one of my favorites. He doesn't profess to be a strong runner, although he's run vastly longer distances than I have. The secret to doing this, he claims, is to go as slow as you need to so you can continue.

This advice has saved me when both running and writing. It's the best approach going for the groaning on the landing before you reach home moment. Or the point when you know there are a few more chapters to go, but you're so tired you no longer feel connected to the story.

SLOWING down isn't the same as giving up. Adjust your tempo so you can get your breath back. Look at the pace you've been keeping up to this point and cut it in half. Did your critic just hiss inside your head? Good. That means it was a big enough chop.

It's important to remember that even on the cusp of proving you can finish this book, the critic is still fighting against your getting it done. It's still trying to protect you from seeking publication and potentially facing rejection in the process. When you're just about to finish, pushing you to the point of burnout where you can't continue at all is sometimes the last card it has to play. Don't let it tell you to work to the point of wiping yourself out when the end is so close.

There are many ways to slow your pace so you can breathe again. Write for less time the same number of days you usually write per week. Cut one day entirely. Or, if you're on the floor groaning and start crying, take a few days off.

I know. This feels counterproductive. Taking a rest stop so you can cross the finish line with your head held high is not giving up. It's good self-care, but you need to check in often to avoid losing focus entirely. Take one day off and see how your energy feels tomorrow. If you still feel flattened, take another day. Once you feel the glimmer return that says you're excited again, or at least feel the possibility of forward movement, don't go in at full speed. Take a gentle step in. As soon as that feels manageable, increase speed slightly, perhaps ten to fifteen percent. Don't double your efforts, as this will land you back in the same state as before. This approach is infuriating to the ego, who wants to go faster and faster until you can cross this draft off the list. It will still happen if you pace yourself well.

BUILDING a writing life isn't about pushing yourself into complete collapse to finish projects. If you like writing books, presumably this isn't the only one you want to complete. Set yourself up so you can bounce back more easily after getting to the end. Even if you've written the final draft of the book, there is always another step waiting, whether that's submitting it, or moving on to marketing if it's already set to get published.

When you hit the Nine of Wands line, knowing you're close to empty, take replenishing seriously. When you cut down your writing time, don't let busywork or other draining activities take that time back. Reallocate your extra time left over from shorter writing sessions to nourishing your creative self. This might look like reading, gentle exercise, a walk, or even just a nap. Keep track of what makes you feel better when you're run down and spend time on one of those activities when it feels like a grind to work on your writing at the pace you'd been maintaining up to that point.

OUR DESIRE TO get to the end point can cause us to value speed over everything else. But remember, if you're writing for pleasure there is no prize for being more frazzled when you finish your book. Being a fast writer doesn't necessarily equate to being pleased with the books that result from those quick efforts. If you invest more into a satisfying process that sometimes goes slower than your ego would like, you stand to gain hugely in quality of work as well as your mental health. And in most cases, the shift in timeline is minimal. Don't let your critic tell you all is lost if you finish a few days or weeks later than planned. Having a book you're happy with is worth taking that time.

QUESTIONS TO PONDER:

- What is your current timeline goal for completing your book?
- Does it make you feel calm or panicked?
- What would it mean to you if getting to the end took longer?
- What shifts in your schedule would make you feel more in control of how the process was going?
- What are you telling yourself about how writers should work that needs to be investigated?

22

TEN OF WANDS

THE PREVAILING fantasy for writers is of toiling away alone in a cabin in the woods in the snow, wearing a torn sweater, cup of coffee steaming on the desk beside us. While it's true that much of writing takes place alone, this can push us to complete exhaustion.

If you turn to the back of any book and read the acknowledgments section, which I recommend making a regular practice of, you'll see that books don't get produced by one person alone in most cases. It is possible to do this today, but not necessary.

When in the rush of a new idea, there is plenty of creative juice to keep you motivated to continue writing. But as the process continues, this can be harder to call up. Books take a long time, much longer than this rush of initial inspiration lasts. It takes one village to keep you fired up to write, and another to get the book into print.

Worrying that you don't have what it takes to finish this thing is a reasonable fear. We see in the Ten of Wands that the figure has taken on far more of a load than they can carry alone. While in most cases we have to write without support, we don't have to stay inspired in a vacuum.

IF YOU'RE scared you can't get to the end of a book, one of the best antidotes is co-working. A favorite part of my annual writing membership has come to be our weekly study halls. We get on a video call together, share what we're working on, and then write for an hour on mute, usually with cameras on. The simple fact of knowing others are there writing with us keeps us motivated to continue. Full disclosure: I wrote about ninety percent of this book in these study halls. And just this morning, one member said she was very tired and didn't want to join today, but had showed up because she knew she'd feel better afterward if she wrote. Showing up when you don't feel like it gets books written, so whatever you can do to make starting less of an effort will serve you well.

There are many ways this can look. I know people who've set up a regular call with a friend to write. There are also organizations like the London Writers' Salon, which offers regular group writing sessions in time zones around the world. Much of the appeal of writing in cafes seems to be working near others. When you write with others, you don't have to carry quite so much up the hill yourself.

IN ADDITION, there are aspects of writing that aren't our strongest points. Perhaps you're a wonderful writer but not as confident at research. This is another area where you can enlist the support of others. Building a relationship with a research librarian or reaching out to your community to see if there's an expert you can interview on a particular topic is a way to put down some of those heavy wands rather than carrying them all alone.

If you publish traditionally, wands get distributed once your book gets sold. You have an editor, a cover designer, interior designer, and marketing and PR to help produce and sell the book. These days, the author carries a lot more weight than in the past, but some of the burden is shifted. If you publish independently, it's tempting to try to do it all yourself. If you have the resources available, try to ask for help. Hiring experts to design your cover, proofread, and lay out your book for publication makes a huge difference, and gives your book a better chance of success. Don't do everything by yourself.

Pay attention to your language about your project. The belief that you have to do it all yourself tends to sneak up on you. Watch yourself if you start thinking you need to learn new software or design programs or tell yourself this one extra thing will be fine for you to take on.

BEING a writer is a wonderful opportunity to learn new skills, if you genuinely want to do so. But forcing yourself to become a graphic designer, editor, and book formatter in order to publish your book is a lot to ask. And please, oh please, do not try to proofread your own work. By the time you send a book to publish or submit to agents you'll have read those pages dozens, if not hundreds of times. You are no longer sensitive enough to see any typos or mistakes you might have made. Given that we find these in professionally published books that have been proofed through multiple rounds, it's pretty much guaranteed you'll let more errors slip through working on your own work. Don't carry that burden.

IF YOU'RE afraid to put down all this weight because of financial constraints, know that there are ways to reduce the cost of getting help. Swap proofreading with a friend who's also finishing a manuscript. Better to read someone else's work as you'll each catch more than you would on your own pages. If you don't have the resources to hire someone for an original cover, look for templates you can adapt rather than starting entirely from scratch on your own.

As independent people, writers often want to do it all ourselves, but this wears us out fast. Put those wands down and ask for help. This doesn't make you less of a writer, nor does it make the book any less yours. You want the book to shine, so accept support to find any mistakes and correct them before it goes out in the world. This is the best investment of money or time you can make in your book. Promise.

To offset the Ten of Wands fear, regularly ask yourself if you are the best person to be doing any new book-related tasks that come up. Be sure to reflect on whether you want to do these new tasks as well. You don't have to do it all, and it's best not to if you want to keep writing more books. Spend as much time on writing and the tasks you love as you can, and hand off the wands that feel the heaviest. Write in connection with others to get more books written in less time. This is the way to get up that mountain without collapsing.

———

AS WE ARRIVE at the end of the Wands, we have seen the full progression of fear of having enough motivation to persevere all the way to the point when we're clutching hold of more responsibility than we can manage.

Throughout the Wands, paying attention to your energy levels is a good indicator about how the process is going. We want to keep things fiery and often choose the most dramatic option, working toward being celebrated because our culture has told us so many times that this is what we should be motivated by.

But as you've followed the path of the Wands, my hope is that you have a much better sense of what actually motivates you, regardless of external messages. Follow the impulses that truly light you up and you'll have the energy of the Wands on your side.

QUESTIONS TO PONDER:

- What, if anything, have you taken on to complete your book that doesn't feel good?
- What help do you wish you had for your writing?

- What skills do you enjoy using as part of writing?
- Which ones do you wish someone else would take over?
- What can you surrender right now?

23

SWORDS OVERVIEW

FEAR THAT GRIPS you in the middle of the night, racing thoughts screaming: This is realm of the Swords. All the fears that live in the mind. We feel these as a running monologue, incessant questions, doubts, nagging suspicions, and the critic's list of rules. These don't come from the gut, they come from the head.

The desire to figure things out as if the mind were in full control drives these fears. This is a lie. We writers live in our heads, and being able to imagine worlds and translate them into pages of story is a powerful skill. But just because we work with our minds doesn't mean our minds are the only tool we have. The idea that you think through the whole book to solve every question in your head before beginning to write is nonsense. The critic wants you to believe this is the most effective approach, but it doesn't improve your writing, it causes you to freeze, trapped in preparation forever.

. . .

WE LEARN SO MUCH about the book in the process of writing it and we need to trust that we will find the answers we need as we work. The fear that we don't know what we're doing is the underlying terror of the Swords. We believe that we must get our minds around all the details or else we will fail.

The Swords want you to have everything neatly laid out with all details decided, like an architect with every electrical line and window pre-planned. But writing is more flexible than this. It can bend and change, more like a living thing growing than an architectural construction. As we work through the fears of the Swords, you'll sort through the thoughts that help you and the ones that hold you back.

The planning and thinking can tangle you up in a barbed-wire net very quickly, so we'll take this suit slowly. When you feel your mind taking over, preventing your connection to anything but your thoughts, take deep breaths, feel your body on the surface where you're sitting, or put your feet on the floor if that's available. Look around the room and let your eyes land on objects in the space. Label what you see in the moment: lamp, window, table, rug. Bring yourself back to the present, away from the whirling energy of the mind.

You are more than your thoughts, despite what the critic tells you. We can make our thoughts our friends with this process, and on the other side, I hope your vision will feel more expansive. Let's begin our trip through our mental maze and see what we discover.

24

ACE OF SWORDS

AS WE ENTER OUR MINDS, the Ace is the first slice of the Swords. Whereas we fear having enough emotion or motivation with the Cups and Wands, the fear as we enter the Swords centers on our intelligence.

Writers, skilled with words as we are, often use them unkindly toward ourselves. And when we find an idea that's going to take a lot of mental skill, our fear is that we aren't up to the challenge.

Having written a novel that took me over five years, I was wiped out. The effort of sustaining enthusiasm for the characters and the story felt quite high. A few months after finishing this book and beginning to query it, a new idea popped into my head.

But instead of merely a historical plot thread, this idea was dual-timeline, with one of the sections taking place in a heavily researched historical era. It also involved reinterpreting the lives of several well-known historical figures. I sat with the massive amount of work I knew this would take, and the Ace of Swords fears snuck in the door.

"You're not a historian — clearly you can't write this book."

"You're going to be a laughingstock. How can you manage something this audacious when you never even got a history degree?"

THIS WAS FAR from my first face-off with my critic. When the critic starts throwing objections in the face of an idea, I know I'm on to something. Our critics get threatened when we start a project that can have an impact on us, and on readers. From now on, trust that a panicked critic means you've hit something juicy.

Not that this feels good in the moment. If your critic starts hurling insults at you and doubting your education, experience, reputation, or intelligence being enough to write the book, that's the stab of the Swords. The critic itself is a very Sword-heavy experience: our mind attacking our own mind. Ouch.

The Swords are the most funhouse-feeling of the fears because they're the hardest to reason your way out of. If your mind is subsumed with a voice insulting your intelligence and skill as a writer, there's not much room to think about anything else. The shift we need to make with Swords-based fears is to put space between yourself and the thoughts.

. . .

IF YOUR MIND IS WHIRRING, telling you that you don't have what it takes to write this book, that the idea is above your level of talent or ability, don't try to fight back with words. The critic loves to debate and will always respond to any point you make with "But..." followed by another argument. It doesn't care if its points are logical either. All it cares about is stopping you from writing.

If you get into a mental loop of arguing with your critic, the back and forth can go on indefinitely. The critic is never satisfied, so you're never going to have the mic drop moment of your dreams where you tell it why you are destined to write this book and it replies, "Of course you are — go for it!"

If we think of a Sword as a dangerously sharp blade, the best way to handle it is with protection. Think of knights wearing armor to prevent getting run through during battle.

SHIFTING into another state is the most effective way to distance yourself from the Ace of Swords, and most of the Sword-based fears, as we'll discuss in the coming chapters. What I mean by another state is another way of relating to your experience. Swords relate to the world through the mind, so a shift away from the Swords state could be drawing or nonverbal art-making, a physical activity like movement, dance, exercise like walking or running, or simply pausing to breathe. If you have a meditation practice, the change we're looking for is the one that comes when you can watch your thoughts move past without immediately claiming them as yours.

Your mind isn't the only authority in your writing or your life, no matter how much the critical part of your mind wants you to believe this. You aren't inherently capable or incapable of writing a particular idea. You may have more or less experience with a particular type of writing, but writing is a skill, and skills can be learned and improved.

In fact, the point when you are least qualified to write a particular book is always right at the beginning. It's the process of actually writing the book that makes you capable of writing it. Every book teaches you new skills. Some of those skills come quickly, and some take years, like the novel I mentioned above.

ONCE I STEPPED BACK and connected with the messages outside my mind telling me I wasn't smart enough, I realized what was actually true was that I didn't have the energy or motivation for a minimum-five-year project right off the back of one that had taken that same amount of time.

I wasn't lacking in intelligence or training; I was lacking the desire to write it then. It just didn't light me up in that moment. I did some preliminary work to make sure, and then confirmed my impressions and set the book aside. But it's still waiting for me if I feel the call again later.

It's important not to let a fear of not being smart enough stand unchallenged. It would have felt terrible to walk away from that novel believing I wasn't qualified to write it. Looking more closely and realizing I didn't want to write it just then was a much more empowering choice.

A nice trick to look underneath fears the critic levels at you is The Work by Byron Katie, a process that is fully explained in her book, *Loving What Is*. It's a series of questions she developed for personal inquiry and growth, but I have found them to be equally effective with writing, particularly dealing with the critic and fearful thoughts.

THESE ARE HER QUESTIONS:

- Is it true?
- Can you absolutely know that it's true?
- How do you react, what happens, when you believe that thought?
- Who would you be without the thought?

Adjusting them to suit our needs in writing, I prefer the final question to read

"What would you do next without the thought?"

———

ONCE WE REALIZE we have choices even though these fears and thoughts arise, there is so much more room to breathe, and to write. Take one fear at a time — for example, "I'm not smart enough to write this book" — and explore it in your journal using the questions laid out above.

Exploring this in the example I shared above, I might have written that I didn't feel smart enough due to my lack of formal training, but in response to the second I'd have to admit that I couldn't absolutely know I wasn't smart enough to write the book. When I believed that thought I felt forced to write it to prove to myself that I was able to, but once I considered who I'd be without the thought, I was able to see that I didn't have to write this book to prove anything to myself. I could choose a new project that was just as exciting to me as my previous novel was.

By looking deeper into the fears of the Swords, you'll become clear enough to make a decision that feels right for you.

25

TWO OF SWORDS

WHEN YOU BEGIN WRITING and the idea is fresh, the world opens up. Everything feels possible. The excitement is palpable, driving you ahead with a reverberating yes. This intoxicating phase lasts until that fateful day when you reach... a decision point.

Those of us who grew up on Robert Frost's "The Road Not Taken" freeze up when we reach the story's first crossroads. After all, in that poem there was clearly a "correct" choice. The one that was different, unique, transformational. But which one is it?

IN A NOVEL, there are thousands of decisions to make. Where the story's set, the challenges the character faces and how they react in these moments, the other characters they encounter, and each point in the plot and character arcs all the way to the end. Every time we say yes to one option, we must say no to another. It is at this point the fear kicks in.

"What if I've made the wrong choice?"

I've seen this play out hundreds of times. The doubt that creeps in removes clarity and destabilizes you. The fear of the "wrong" choice can paralyze you. I've seen writers stuck in this trap for months and even years. It's debilitating.

HOWEVER, this fear, like many of the others, is built on yet another unhelpful metric: that of finding the "right" choice. The right choice doesn't exist, because there is no way to confirm you've found it. There is a little gang of nasty voices in your head, and trying to get a useful picture of how your work is progressing based on their input is impossible. If you find yourself asking if this is the right choice, if the story is gaining momentum, or if you worry you've made the wrong choice, you're stuck. If you remember the film *The Neverending Story*, and the terrifying scene where Artax's horse gets sucked down into the swamp of sadness, you'll have a good idea of what this fear is capable of. It won't kill you physically, but it can destroy your creative spirit and your confidence in yourself, which is a death of another kind.

THE PROBLEM WITH THE GOOD/BAD right/wrong unique/cliched or derivative polarities is that they are all subjective. There is nothing everyone on Earth can point to and agree is good writing. Nor bad, nor unique. Even if we try to go all the way back to cave drawings as a unique expression, we can't, because there are patterns between sites all around the world. Stories have patterns too, marked out by archetypes and story structures we witness all the way back to Ancient Greece and prehistoric times.

Trying to make a choice with your brain to find the mythical correct choice could distract you for the rest of your life, if you let it. Meanwhile you have no book. This is why the critic deploys this nasty seed of doubt — it's effective in making you run round in circles.

Please accept that these are unhelpful to ask about your work. Acting as if there is an objective ideal gives you nothing to navigate with. It's a bit like being dropped in the middle of a desert with no landmarks and a blank map, being told that you should know where you're going, and if you don't — it's already too late.

THE REASON these polarities shut you down is that they don't give you anything to navigate with. They pretend not to be subjective, all the while hiding the most subjective agenda of all. "Good" is a construct of the time and place and culture it exists within. Look at fashion and, in particular, hairstyles. How many times have you looked through old photos and cringed at images of yourself wearing a piece of clothing or haircut you felt great in at the time, that you now wish you could travel back in time to prevent yourself from choosing? Were you right in the past, feeling great, or are you right now, feeling embarrassed?

This is true of art and literature as well. Trends come and go. Try reading a book from twenty or thirty years ago right next to a book that's just come out. There are so many shifts. Things that were acceptable to write in the past are now clearly inappropriate and we'd never write them. And, at the same time, when I read older books I'm struck at differences in pacing and structure that can make a book feel like it was written on another planet, let alone in another decade.

Trying to build your foundation on top of correct choices means you're trying to build a solid structure on top of a rushing river. It's never going to hold.

What can you do instead?

Embrace the subjectivity of writing. Bake it in to the questions you ask to assess how your writing is going.

INSTEAD OF ASKING "IS this the right choice?" questions like these point you in a meaningful direction:

- Does this feel engaging?
- Does this scene contain the events I wanted to include?
- Do I feel connected to the character now?
- Am I satisfied with this?
- Do I want to keep going?
- Does this convey the atmosphere and emotional experience I wanted to portray?

DO you see how these questions contain criteria you can engage meaningfully with, rather than a vague ideal no one can measure? Of course we want people to read our writing and think it's well done, but that isn't something we can measure when we write it. It's a byproduct of asking questions like the ones above.

When you take the time to determine what a satisfying finished manuscript would look and feel like and ask questions leading toward those goals, making decisions becomes much easier.

Whereas asking if something is the right choice could shut you down forever, asking whether your character being faced with obstacle A or B would better illustrate their fear of trusting other people is a question you can actually answer.

The critic loves to hit you with vague, unanswerable questions. They will run this playbook as long as they can. Keep asking if you can actually answer the questions that occur to you while writing and you'll be able to sort the useful ones from the critic's freeze rays before long.

As Rachael Stephen, author of *State of Flux* and creator of the Story Magic Academy points out, "maybe" is a useless answer when faced with a decision. It's better to make the wrong choice and keep writing than to try to continue without making the choice at all.

Come up with more helpful metrics to guide your choices, make the best choice you can, and move forward. If the choice doesn't work, you'll know, and then you can adjust. But freezing or not moving ahead at all will steal your chance to finish your book.

If we return to Robert Frost, the road less traveled in writing isn't the difference between A and B for any of the individual choices you're faced with. The road less traveled is making the choices knowing you can't be entirely certain in the outcome. Trusting yourself to navigate without proof is the skill that will get you through the book.

Make your choices. Trust yourself. This is the way to end up with a finished book.

26

THREE OF SWORDS

THE GOAL of writing is most often to connect with a reader, making them deeply relate to the words we've put on the page. But in order to do so, we have to share things that scare us. The fear of being vulnerable is one that comes to all writers, especially when we dig deep. This is the Three of Swords.

While at first glance this looks like a fear that belongs with the Cups, given the need to be vulnerable, the source of the fear is that our words and thoughts on the page will come back to stab us in the heart. The aftermath may be emotional, but the cause is absolutely mental. When we translate our innermost feelings and impulses into writing, either for fiction or nonfiction, we risk exposure and heartbreak. This is scary.

IN THE RECENT FRENCH FILM, *Anatomy of a Fall*, this tension plays out in full force onscreen. The main character, a novelist, is accused of pushing her husband out a window, causing his death. As part of the trial, the opposing attorney reads excerpts of her fiction, claiming that her writing about homicidal impulses in her books revealed a desire to kill her husband.

Every writer I've talked to about this moment was horrified. What we write is meant to be sacred. Fiction is based on "what if" questions we play out in our minds. The thought that I could one day be put on trial for experiments I'd undertaken in stories was enough to scare me off from writing for a few days.

It's reasonable to worry that what you write will come back to haunt you. Hopefully, this won't include being on trial for murder, but the fear that it's dangerous to reveal our less savory sides is understandable.

Whether you are bracing for attacks from internet trolls, being misunderstood, attacked or rejected, trying to anticipate other people's reactions to your book while you're still writing it is a prescription for freezing up. I won't say you shouldn't filter or consider the potential consequences of your work. Speaking up and sharing can rock the boat, and you get to decide what others read.

However, separating the writing from the sharing can help you get clear on what feels safe to publish and what doesn't. Writing a raw scene that exposes you completely is worth doing. Just because you've written it doesn't mean anyone else has to see it. I've found that writing it is important. When we start turning away from ideas because we're afraid they might be too much for others, without even exploring them, we make our writing smaller.

. . .

IF WE DON'T REVEAL ENOUGH, if we don't go to the roots of a topic in our writing, we may regret that later on. Zadie Smith, interviewed years ago on Bookworm for KCRW in Los Angeles, shared the experience of re-reading her novel *The Autograph Man* years later, after having published multiple books in the meantime. She found moments when she could have gone deeper, and these nagged at her:

> *"When I write badly, it's because I've been cowardly — I've lied. It seems odd to say in fiction I've lied, but any writer knows what I'm talking about. I can re-read a book like I re-read* The Autograph Man *on a plane for the first time a few days ago. And I was enjoying it [up] to a point that I got to a twenty-page section and I knew it was a lie.*
>
> *And I remember when I wrote it, I knew it was a lie. That's what I mean. It's very, very hard to discuss as a critic or as an academic. But writers know what I'm talking about. And it's one of the most profound feelings of self-betrayal. You've betrayed yourself in some way."*

THE CHALLENGE of the Three of Swords is to expose our emotional depths enough so we do the story and the characters justice. The same with memoir, which is its own complex dance.

Letting our writing break our hearts first is the best way to reach the reader deeply, but this means we have to become resilient. We need to take good care of ourselves. The myth of the starving artist, freezing cold in the attic, doesn't serve this kind of writing. If you're torturing yourself in the process of writing, it's very hard to write vulnerable material without falling apart. Working this way leads to self-destruction. We see it in substance abuse throughout the history of artists and writers. Tolerating vulnerability and building a workable way to be in hard places for yourself and your characters is an ongoing practice.

YOU WON'T GET it right immediately. It's ok to go slow. It's ok to keep asking how it would feel if others read the scene *this* way. Sometimes a slight shift is all it takes to keep the emotion without pushing you past what you can tolerate.

But writing all the way through the depths can be healing, too. Separate these two parts. You're allowed to write for yourself first. Yes, the goal is to share the book with readers, but until you send it out, the book is yours.

Taking gradual steps can help here, too. An editor, first reader, or another writer you trust can be a helpful second pair of eyes on the question. Balancing intensity in stories is a lot like balancing the soundtrack to a film.

It's rarely a question of music or no music, but rather a delicate process of turning individual instruments up or down, and then the entire piece of music can support the story.

LET THERE BE NUANCE HERE. Let it be an ongoing conversation you have with yourself. And above all, try different approaches before you shut down a storyline or a scene. Don't rush to decide if they belong or not. We are the least clear-eyed about our writing immediately after putting it on the page. I've written things many times I thought were garbage, only to return a few days or weeks later and realize I could work with them just fine.

Take the time you need. Trust yourself and trust your story to find your way through. And know that every writer feels this fear with you. All our hearts can be broken, so treat your own gently, while also knowing you are brave enough to use your words to share the emotional truth, which is the most healing of all.

QUESTIONS TO PONDER:

- What are you afraid will happen if you are vulnerable in your writing?
- Where do you want to go deeper in what you share?
- How can you connect more with potential readers?

- What small step could you take toward sharing more?
- Who can you show you work to as a test run?
- What would you include in the story, if you knew it would be received in the spirit it was written?

27

FOUR OF SWORDS

"WRITE EVERY DAY." Much of the advice in well-known books champions this method above all others. "Real writers write daily." Similar to "real writers get up at 5am" — or earlier — and don't need sleep like mere mortals.

If you, like me, are the sort of person who has zero useful ideas at 5am and tends to run out of gas after several days of focused writing, you may be plagued by the fear of the Four of Swords: the fear of taking a break.

HABIT APPS that create a chain of successful writing days are hugely motivating in many contexts. Seeing a solid line of checkmarks makes most of us feel like champions. But what happens when you get sick, or your kid gets sick, or your day job gets busy? Once the chain gets broken, it may feel impossible to get your rhythm back or even to begin again at all.

This is the shadow side of the "write every single

damned day" approach. Yes, writing consistently makes a huge difference. But writing consistently and writing daily aren't necessarily the same thing. During lockdown, I played around with many schedules, and in working with hundreds of students, I've seen countless incarnations of sustainable writing routines. Nearly all of them include rest.

REST IS NOT THE ENEMY. In fact, planning rest into your schedule often creates a more successful result over time. Writing a book is a long-haul project. You can write an essay in a sprint of a few days or a week, and blog posts in less time than that, but a book doesn't happen in a week. My priority is a long life writing many books, so planning to write them without getting burned out is essential.

What allowed me to write without the fear of everything falling apart if I took a break was to plan those breaks as part of the schedule. This has worked well for students and clients as well. When I've run my novel-drafting intensive, Dream to Draft, we write Monday through Friday and take weekends off. Some people opt to shift the days they rest, but rest is part of the deal.

IF YOU ARE TERRIFIED your book will blow away in the wind if you step away even for a day, perhaps this image will help: think of writing and resting as the exhale and the inhale. When you're writing the book, you're exhaling your ideas onto the page. Transforming your ideas into sentences and paragraphs and chapters is an exhale. But no one can exhale forever without taking in fresh air and oxygen. Your rest days are your inhale. I'm not suggesting that you forget the book completely during those rest days, although sometimes a day completely away helps a lot. When I write, I take weekends off, and usually spend extra time reading, watching a film or show, or spending time with friends and family. This is my inhale. Anything that builds inspiration or sparks new ideas counts as an inhale. I've gone to bookshops or museums, or worked on creative hobbies, like sewing and knitting, to inhale new ideas that then fuel me when I return to the book after the pause. I've come to depend on these inhale breaks, and realize that refueling means the book gets written more quickly and more enjoyably.

This is a tricky habit to put in place, but every writer I've spoken to has benefited from setting parameters and resting on purpose regularly. This might be one week in the midst of a longer writing stretch, or for some it means still writing daily, but writing a lot less per day. My method of weekends off isn't the be-all and end-all, but hopefully it gives you something to respond to.

IF THIS FEELS ENTIRELY NEW, start by keeping a page in your notebook for listing activities that make you feel refreshed or inspired afterward. Perhaps you see a film after not going to the cinema for a long time and find yourself rushing home with a new way to handle a character's backstory. Make a note that the cinema was a good inhale. Or maybe you have that one friend who leaves you buzzing with inspiration every time you meet up. Put them on the list, too.

The point when rest starts to feel scary is when you've left it far too long. If you try to exhale for months without inhaling, you'll get light-headed and won't be able to see straight to continue. If you don't plan for rest you'll be forced into it eventually, in the form of illness, burnout, or losing interest and motivation to continue the project.

There are writers who can churn out a draft in a short period of time, but they do so by leaving their usual routine, often going somewhere they don't have to worry about everyday needs. And this method is time-limited. Perhaps you're a weekend warrior who writes many hours a few days at a time. Follow your natural rhythm, but pay attention to what kind of inhale and replenishment you need after those intense sprints.

For me, even when I go on a writing retreat where I have no other responsibilities, I generally spend two to three hours writing per day and then nap, read, or top up on inspiration the rest of the day. Often, our everyday lives are so busy and filled with demands that we steal time from resting to write. At certain points in life, that will be the choice. However, make sure that you allow for some rest time as often as you can.

THE CONCEPT of the Artist's Date, made popular by Julia Cameron, is a good example of including dedicated inhale time in your schedule. I can't tell you how many times clients and students have followed their curiosity to visit a new neighborhood, museum, or even just parking on a different street only to be rewarded with story gold. The student who parked on a different block than usual in a town she visited frequently got out of the car right next to a shop exactly like the one she'd imagined one of her characters running. She browsed for a bit and then the scenes set there flowed like magic, filled with details she'd seen in the actual shop.

We are incredible creative beings, writers. We create worlds and societies and characters in our books. But we are also humans who run out of energy and fuel after churning out page after page. Plan to take breaks and you'll be able to maintain your writing pace much longer. These breaks don't have to be lying in bed, either. When needed, step away and do something very different if you're worried you can't write that day. Mindless tasks like folding laundry, doing dishes, or admin that use a different part of your brain can function as rest from writing.

THE CRITIC WILL OBJECT at first, calling these breaks a waste of time, but putting replenish days on the calendar and watching the result will soon make their benefit obvious. If need be, reassess daily or weekly what your rest needs are. If the fear of losing your grip on writing gets loud, remind yourself that this plan is only for today, or until a set date in the near future. Check in frequently and honor your needs.

You'll be surprised how delicious writing feels after a conscious pause. Far from breaking your connection to your work, I find it strengthens the work and my commitment to it every time. Take small steps when you begin, and don't expect perfection. Follow your enthusiasm and the energy that's built up in the course of your rest. See what thoughts are most exciting and follow their lead. Absence absolutely makes the heart grow fonder, especially with writing.

QUESTIONS TO PONDER:

- How much sleep do you need to feel rested?
- How much are you currently getting?
- What activities feel like an inhale to you?
- Which one can you schedule in this week?
- What regular inhale practice would feel supportive?

28

FIVE OF SWORDS

IS WRITING a book a selfish way to spend your time? This question nearly always comes up once people realize how much time it actually takes to finish a book.

A similar fear arises when people consider writing memoir. Who would care about their lives, after all? Is it self-indulgent to write about my own life? After all, who would ever care about that?

When we step away from our regular responsibilities to spend time writing, we're making a choice. The time we spend writing could go to laundry or preparing our taxes, or to friends and family. Isn't it incredibly arrogant to shut ourselves away and work on writing instead?

THIS FEAR SEEMS logical at first, but as soon as you start digging, the cracks in its logic appear. Have you noticed that the idea that writing is selfish doesn't extend to other activities that take time away from our responsibilities? No one seems to have the fear "Who am I to post on social media? How dare I take time away from friends and family to post images and write captions about them!" The same goes for activities like sports or other hobbies. I don't hear knitters around the world gnashing their teeth feeling terrible about making sweaters and other crafts. Ditto for those who run or cycle or bake bread.

So what is it about writing or, for that matter, the arts that require time spent alone to work? If it's not about the time spent, then what is it about? Perhaps we could call it guilt over putting so much time into our own creativity, but this doesn't fit either.

All writers ultimately want to share their work with readers. Knitters often give sweaters away, but writers have a lot more power with their creation. I'm never going to knit a sweater that could keep an infinite number of people warm all by itself, but one book can entertain or inspire every person who wants to buy it at the same time. Why is it ok to bake a pie, but not to write books?

ONCE WE DIG below the ideas of wasted time and the benefit our work could provide to others, we get to the core of this fear. If you look at it closely, you aren't afraid that you're being selfish. What you're actually afraid of is never completing the book and therefore producing nothing that could benefit others.

Knitting, sports, gardening, and other activities we spend time on don't create guilt because we can follow a plan and get a predictable result. Writing doesn't work that way. Yes, there are general practices, but writers vary hugely. The plan that helps me write a book may not work for you at all and vice versa. In the absence of a map to follow, we fear that writing is selfish because we can't guarantee a precise result.

If I'm sitting in a room alone, spending time away from my family but never actually finish a book, then is all that time somehow stolen from my loved ones? Let's take this apart and see what's happening underneath:

WOULD you call it a waste if writing made you feel calmer and happier and then passed that energy on to those around you, even if you never finished the book? Is the message about following your dreams an important one you want to pass on? If you do make it clear that being creative is part of a satisfying life, is it really so selfish to take time for your writing?

Obviously, I'm not suggesting you ignore crying babies who need a diaper change, or completely dismiss work deadlines until you lose your income. What I am suggesting is that we all spend time on things for ourselves, but these aren't always the things we actually want to be doing. If you resent not being able to write under your current circumstances, are you telling yourself that writing is selfish, or is this fear a way to avoid taking a close look at what would need to change in order to allow you to write? Would it mean admitting the job isn't working for you or that you'd have to ask your family for support and flexibility?

Being open to the thoughts doesn't mean any action is required, but the critic works fast and tries to shut down any line of thinking it considers dangerous. And it always sees writing as dangerous. The known-but-unsatisfying result of scrolling mindlessly through apps is no risk to the status quo. Sharing with your family that you want to write a book is. Looking at your budget and asking if you could get flex-time at work or share your role in order to go part time is a big change that may have the critic shouting about how reckless you are being.

BUT LIFE ISN'T ONLY about playing it safe. While safety is important, it is more and less essential to us at different stages in our lives. The critic will always put safety and predictable outcomes first, but that doesn't mean you have to agree.

Asking "why?" in response to the critic's assertions is a good start. I also like Martha Beck's version, in her book *The Way of Integrity*: "Are you sure?" As Beck contemplated writing a memoir about leaving the Mormon faith that she accurately predicted would prove explosive, the pressure to maintain the status quo was immense. She received countless threats and consistent pushback for sharing her experience in the church openly, including truths most people did not want to reach the wider world. Even in the face of terror that telling this story was a huge mistake that had left her in danger, she still asked herself "Are you sure?" when those fears came up.

WHENEVER THE CRITIC tells you how to feel about writing, whenever it claims you're deluding yourself about the value of your work, keep asking that voice if it's sure. What if someone had worried they were crazy because their experience in the church wasn't reflected anywhere but found comfort in Beck's book, even years after it was written. Was it a bad idea to write it? She maintains that the benefits have outweighed the risks, for her.

What if your book can reach someone who needs it, even if you don't know who they are or how they'll find it yet? Is it still selfish to take the time you need to get it written? Are you sure?

QUESTIONS TO PONDER:

- Does writing feel selfish to you?
- How would you define selfish?
- What does it mean if you take time for yourself and your own interests?
- How do you feel your writing could benefit others?

29

SIX OF SWORDS

FOLLOWING on the worry that writing is selfish, if we start believing that writing is worth our time and effort, a new fear arises: that writing will turn us into someone else. This makes some sense. If you're worried writing is selfish, but you think it's ok to take time to write, does that mean you've become a selfish person?

The Six of Swords shows a figure crossing a body of water, traveling from one shore to the other. In most desks based on the Rider-Waite-Smith conventions, our figure sits in a small boat with rougher water close to us and calmer water on the other side. This can describe how writing feels when we're struggling. As Dorothy L Parker famously said, "I hate writing. I love having written."

I very much hope that she didn't actually hate writing. But I do agree that when I'm in a tricky stage of a book and it feels like I got nothing done, I'm still always glad I've put time into wrestling with the story afterwards. The more we keep showing up, even if some days are hard, the more worth it the effort feels as pages accu-mulate and we have breakthrough moments. We move through the choppy water and get to the calmer seas on the other side.

IT'S NOT easy to write a book. As a result, it's guaranteed that you will change if you write one. Your entire personality is unlikely to change, but if you knew you could write a book, what else might you believe you're capable of? I've seen countless students ask them-selves this question after completing a draft of a novel or a round of revision, having never realized they were capable of this level of writing before.

In creative fields, the change we fear often gets labeled "selling out." Maybe at first, a creative artist feels free to take risks in their work, but as time passes and perhaps that work becomes the source of their income and security, they're less willing to make waves like the ones we see next to our little boat.

But is this writing changing us? Or is it simply that our priorities as humans change throughout our lives? Wouldn't we have valued security more as time passed whether we wrote or not? There is always a choice. Yes, we have to take care of practical needs, but we can choose whether we want writing to pay the bills, or if we prefer to earn money another way. Writing can be a project we pursue primarily for the enjoyment. Making choices about what we want is part of the process.

If we come to enjoy earning money and supporting ourselves with our writing, does this mean we've sold out?

I don't believe it does. If we enjoy the work we're doing and we feel satisfied with it along with the compensation, this sounds like a fair trade to me. But this is a personal question to consider.

BEING able to write books will change your concept of who you are. Reflect on what you'd feel if you held a finished book of your own in your hands. Do you feel different? And, more importantly, are you happy with this shift? If so, let writing change you. It's ok to be impacted by our experience and to become different people through the creative work we do. After all, if our work had no impact on us, we would need to look at whether there were deeper levels to explore.

EARLY ON IN our writing lives, we may fall prey to the idea of what we should be writing. For example, someone might think it's more valuable to write Literary Fiction, when in reality they'd be much happier writing Science Fiction, Romance, or Mystery. Genre fiction has taken a lot of hits to its reputation, quite unfairly in my opinion, and it can take a long time for us to accept we'd rather write that than force ourselves into a mold that doesn't fit.

The fear of striking out and writing books we love to read is real. I followed literary fiction's guidelines for years before accepting that most of the time what I loved to read was mystery. I'd woven elements of mystery into my first novel, but it didn't entirely reflect the stories that gripped me. It felt scary to shift my course because the publishing world is much more likely to pigeonhole an author now than it did even just twenty years ago. I know one cozy mystery writer who had a darker, grittier story idea and shared it with her agent, only to be told she'd have to write it under a pseudonym, since it was too different from the writing brand she'd already established.

BREAKING free of the rules we have for ourselves about what we should be writing is scary enough, but when we want to break free from rules the publishing and reading world has established, that can be scarier still. We might feel very alone in our little boat, setting our course in an entirely new direction. The thing to remember is that the waves are calmer on the other side.

If you're faced with a choice that feels daunting, like writing in a new way, writing genre rather than literature, or even taking a different direction within the genre you currently write, know you are in good company, and not just among writers. All creatives face this moment.

Remember the musician with a popular album who then writes something in an entirely different tone and is excited to play it on tour, only to face an audience that prefers what it already knows. Or the artist who finally sells work consistently in one style, only to tire of it and long to try something totally different, despite critical backlash. The artist Philip Guston worked in multiple styles throughout his career as a painter. In the early years of his career, he worked in an abstract expressionist style and his representational work drew on classical references. But as he continued to develop as a painter, his work took a drastic turn. Fascinated by the ways evil hid in plain sight in mainstream America, his work took on a cartoonish feel with pointed ghost-like figures, reminiscent of the Ku Klux Klan, featuring heavily.

The backlash was strong with many colleagues and gallerists panning the work as childish and a huge mistake on the artist's part. It's only now that retrospectives are appearing, lauding Guston's exploration of the banality of evil as well ahead of its time. There was rough water to cross, but he was fortunate enough to see people change their minds about his art before his death.

Taking a stand for yourself and your desires as a writer can feel scary at first, but as soon as you commit and set sail, notice how it feels. If you have the sense that you're finally sailing home, you know you've made the choice that's right for you.

QUESTIONS TO PONDER:

- What matters most to me?
- Are you willing to sail to the other side of the water?
- Are you willing to make changes that might make your work more (or less) commercially viable?
- What if you wrote something that looks totally different than what you've tried before?

30

SEVEN OF SWORDS

EARLY ON IN A PROJECT, I'm quiet about what I'm working on. The idea often feels amorphous and having outside input isn't helpful yet. I always want to be completely clear about what I'm writing before I let anyone else comment on it.

However, once I have a foundation, I've found bouncing ideas off other writers and book-loving friends with similar taste is helpful. Not everyone feels the same — some people are terrified to share their ideas at all. Once the book's essence crystallizes, the fear that the idea might be stolen takes hold.

THIS CAN HAPPEN at any stage in the process, from the very beginning to late in the game, where sending out a manuscript to a potential agent causes total paralysis. Having worked months or years on the book and being so close to the concept, the most devastating thing you can imagine might be having someone walk away with your words without giving you credit. This is one of the reasons R.F. Kuang's *Yellowface* has found such a huge audience — even posthumously, having a book stolen without any acknowledgment to the original author gives all of us the creeps.

GIVEN how much we hear about plagiarism, from everything to online articles to excepts of novels sampled and passed off as new work in a number of scandals, it's understandable to want to protect yourself. However, toiling away in obscurity and never talking about your work isn't the best way to protect yourself. Consider well-known authors who've shared their work early and often: Readers knew that *The Martian* was Andy Weir's work because he was posting excerpts frequently and openly. And the reason the 2019 plagiarism scandal, in which Brazilian romance novelist Cristiane Serruya was accused of copying numerous passages of her novels word for word, was uncovered was because fans recognized familiar lines and alerted the original authors.

We can't all guarantee that we'll be household names as writers, but building up a community of people who read and recognize your work is one of the greatest deterrents to plagiarism and theft. The critic is reasonable in wanting to protect you from those who take the easy way out, ripping off other creators, but its strategy is flawed.

BEGIN GENTLY when this fear crops up. When creating a community around your writing, you don't need to begin by sharing all your ideas, or even the content of your projects. You can discuss your process and still make connections with future readers. During 2020, I was revising a novel and wanted some accountability to reach my writing goals, so I began doing livestreams on social media Monday through Friday to share what I was working on that day and how close I was to hitting my writing targets. I didn't share anything about the story, only the nitty gritty of techniques like making index cards to review scenes, the ways I approached my goals, and how I celebrated reaching them. I also explored what happened when I missed a target or needed to redirect the story outline because of discoveries I made while re-writing.

People showed up regularly and shared their own challenges and successes and through these regular sessions, I not only completed my revision, I also built a huge community of people who valued the time and effort it took to rewrite the novel. Through this daily dialogue I built a course, Dream to Draft, which addressed the questions and stuck points members of the community had shared with me. They all know about my books now without my having to reveal anything I wasn't comfortable sharing.

THIS IS ALSO a helpful technique when you're in a social situation, mention you're a writer, and someone asks what your book is about. Scott O'Connor, a teacher of mine, had the best solution I've ever heard to not share anything about the content of your book if you don't want to: Talk about the process, not the content.

Here's how it works. Someone asks, "Oh - what's your novel about?" Respond with the technical details of what you're working on with a vague reference to the plot. "It's a suspense book, and right now I'm working on developing the antagonist. I want to have a villain who's really diabolical, but that people can't help relating to. I'm always fascinated with the human side of people who do terrible things. We can all learn from looking at those sides of ourselves, and I find myself reflecting more when reading fiction than nonfiction." And on from there.

Most people won't notice that you haven't divulged the plot, shifting a philosophical conversation about writing instead. You are not obligated to share anything about your book when people ask. At the same time, discussing your writing in a way that feels safe to you means a community can protect those ideas with you. Yes, keeping manuscripts in a drawer forever may mean no one can steal the content, but as we'll see later in this book, it's no guarantee against someone writing something similar at some point in the future. After all, human experience is archetypal. We all feel fear and sadness and joy, there are rites of passage most of us experience at similar ages, and our global society reads much of the same news, even though people may interpret events differently. We are all pulling ideas from similar sources. So it might not be theft if someone else ends up with a very similar story. It may be that you held back from sharing it so long that someone else came up with an idea that feels a lot like yours.

. . .

FINDING ways to talk about your writing publicly and upping your comfort levels with visibility is an essential skill for any writer. Yes, some people have ulterior motives, but establishing yourself as a writer interested in certain themes and focused on particular genres is the best investment you can make in yourself and your ideas.

Ease into it, test your boundaries, and check in with this fear. It will be a balancing act, but it's worth the risk. Go slow, but keep moving forward. The ultimate goal is to get your books to readers, and the time to begin getting comfortable speaking about your writing starts long before pub day. Take a small step, reflect and repeat.

QUESTIONS TO PONDER:

- What is your worst fear about someone stealing your ideas?
- If you weren't scared that someone would steal your idea, what would you do next?
- Who do you feel comfortable talking about writing with?
- How could you challenge yourself to be more visible as a writer?

31

EIGHT OF SWORDS

BEFORE WE BEGIN LOOKING at this fear, I must confess that the Eight of Swords is my favorite Minor Arcana card. I hope by the end of discussing the fear connected with it, you'll understand why. I was a very shy and anxious kid when I was young, and my imagination had a tendency to take any scary situation and make it worse with the story my mind told me about what was happening.

I accidentally went to a bake sale table at the wrong time, picking out a cupcake before my lunch table had been called. When I sat down where my classmates were still waiting, my mind started telling me how awful I was. "Now everyone will think you're a selfish person," my mind buzzed.

It was as if each scary thought plaguing me was a bee inside my mind. The longer I sat there, no longer interested in the cupcake at all, the more bees appeared.

. . .

OUR FEARS about writing work the same way. Early on, one idea buzzes around in your mind, perhaps something like "Not sure I can do this" or "This isn't working." As you keep working, the fears build and build, forming a giant swarm.

"What was I thinking? I have no idea what I'm doing. This was a terrible idea. I can't write a book. I should stop now before this gets any worse." It feels like a buzzing mass of evidence that you are on the wrong path. After all, who are you to dare to write a book?

You may be asking now why this card, of all the cards in the Minor Arcana, is my favorite. The answer lies in the secret of the nasty messages threatening to sting you.

JUST BECAUSE THEY **are phrased like they're your own internal monologue, doesn't mean they are.**

One of the internal critic's cleverest tricks is to pose as your actual thoughts. In reality, the critic is an accumulation of hurtful feedback we've gotten, or believe we've gotten, throughout our lives. This is the next step of putting distance between ourselves and the thoughts.

For example, a teacher says we don't know how to create a strong sentence in third grade. Despite our having had decades of life experience and chances to strengthen our sentences, there is still a thought reverberating in our head: "I can't write good sentences." Over time, we collect these memories and record them in our minds as if they were accurate assessments that remain true today.

. . .

REMEMBER the person in the one writing class you dared to take who thought your characters "lacked depth"? The one who said this even though they prefer an entirely different type of story to the kind you write? That belief gets immortalized as "I'm bad at character," without any context or taking account what you've learned since. The critic takes the most hurtful aspect and saves it. As a result, we hold out-of-date and inaccurate opinions about our abilities, based on these former judgments.

———

IF YOU DO an image search on the Eight of Swords, the truth this card reveals will be easier to see. The Japaridze tarot has one of my favorites: a woman sits inside a prison cell, eyes downcast, resigned to being trapped inside forever. However, if you look closer, you will see what she doesn't: a key rests in the lock on the inside of the door, waiting for her to notice that she can unlock it and escape whenever she wants.

The key that calls off the swarm of bees for you? The knowledge that the sting of the critic isn't coming from inside your own mind. These are beliefs that someone else held about you in the past. This doesn't make them the truth. If you could speak to your teacher today, it's highly unlikely that she'd remember you as "that student who was destined never to write a good sentence."

The reason I love this card is that it's a reminder that

whatever I believe about my project that's making me feel hopeless is based on flawed evidence. The fear that's shutting you down isn't informed by the facts.

AS SOON AS you realize that you've been sucked into an Eight of Swords vortex, step back. Take a breather from actual manuscript writing for the day. Instead, your time is better spent untangling the false beliefs that are shutting you down. Continuing to write without separating your awareness from your critic's is like navigating with a broken compass: you'll just go in circles, never making real progress.

The first step is to write down as much of the monologue running in your head as you can. I prefer handwriting for this process, but choose whatever form suits you best. If it's easier to speak aloud, another great method to get these out is dictating and then transcribing the audio file. See the resources in the back of this book for options.

I recommend setting a timer when documenting your fears. Go for ten or fifteen minutes and get as much of the recurring loop out on the page or into the recorder as you can. Once you're finished, get up from your chair and, if it's possible for you, shake your body, jump up and down, or move around in some way. Taking a shower or bath is another great way to shift out of this headspace. Other options are going for a walk, listening to music, or playing or cuddling with a pet.

Leave the beliefs aside for a few hours or a day. When you come back to them, do so with your deerstalker hat on, like Sherlock. Read one belief at a time and ask the following questions:

- Do I remember anyone saying this to me? If so, who? When did they say it?
- If there isn't a specific person, is there a voice associated with this belief?
- How old do they sound?
- Do they have a gender?
- What other aspects of their character can I identify?
- Is there any concrete, impartial evidence that this belief is true about my writing now? (Not when this belief first popped up.)
- What resources do I have to assess the truth of this statement?
- If there is any truth at all to it, what can I do about it?

THE CHALLENGE of the Eight of Swords, and the critic overall, is to sort the purely false beliefs that camp out in our minds from the merely out-of-date ones. Finally we can consider those that have some truth to them but are linked to a catastrophic outcome.

For example, "I can't write dialogue so I should just give up writing fiction." Perhaps a teacher or writing friend told you that your dialogue was a bit awkward. We need to separate this comment from what the critic is making it mean. It doesn't immediately follow that struggling with dialogue means you are categorically forbidden to write fiction. A more useful next step would be to focus on learning how to write conversations that feel satisfying on the page.

PLENTY OF WRITERS struggle with dialogue, description, world-building, plot twists and many other writing skills. The trick is not to see this as a death sentence for your writing life. Instead, we can take this as an opportunity to grow as writers.

What if you embraced this part of yourself instead?

"Dialogue is a challenge for me." How does that statement feel compared to "I can't write dialogue so I should just give up writing"? Less of a sting, right?

Now that you've determined what truth there is to the statement, we come to the final step: what can you do about it?

This will, of course, depend on your specific challenge, but overall I find the following tremendously useful in most cases:

- Ask yourself which writers excel at this skill. Who do you wish you could write dialogue like?
- Read this author's work and look more closely at what impresses you most about it. Is their dialogue short and snappy? Genuine and heartfelt? Funny? Take note of how it's written and formatted.

- Keep paying attention to the skill you want to improve when you read. Notice when you don't like an author's choices. If you hate the dialogue in a book, what is it you find unsatisfying? Is there a way to change it so you like it more?

AS YOU READ through the monologue that's been living in your head, you'll find a whole range of beliefs. Not all of them will reveal any truth. Some of them will feel silly the moment you see them written out. That's an incredibly satisfying part of this process — watching the fears that have held you hostage fall away.

By empowering yourself to confront the beliefs lurking in your mind, you'll be able to escape the prison and step outside the trap of the Eight of Swords. After all, a fear we can take concrete action to solve is a fear that can no longer control us.

This isn't a one and done process. Do what you can this first round and then return to your writing. The bees will swarm in the future, but when they do, you'll be ready. After all, you know the key is inside the door now, so you'll never be quite as trapped again.

32

NINE OF SWORDS

THE NINE OF Swords is one of the cards people want to shove right back in the deck the moment they pull it. Part of the issue is its scary name: "The nightmare card." The fear that comes with this card, is just that: that our project has become a nightmare we can't escape.

As with most of the beliefs we've explored so far, we can see the seed of this fear in the preceding cards. With the Eight of Swords, we had the chance to review the negative beliefs about ourselves that haunt us when we write. It's hard work to sort through those fears and determine which ones are no longer valid, but the alternative is the nightmare of those fears running wild and unchecked.

Hitting a wall while writing a book is inevitable, as is the case with any long-term project. Our thoughts cycle through a loop that begins in excitement and bottoms out with dread before we return to the beginning again. It's a roller coaster writers know well.

. . .

THE NIGHTMARE APPEARS when we are drowning in doubt, self-criticism, and dread. I find this moment comes when I'm tired and have been grinding away at a problem in the book the same way for too long. When I wrote my previous novel, I went through multiple drafts struggling with what the love interest's current job was. In one draft he drove a cab, in another he co-owned a bicycle shop, and in a third he had no job at all because I decided not to mention it. This was a disaster as all the tension evaporated, given that he was always available and had no motivation of his own.

I remember sitting at the dinner table with my husband, crying that I'd spent years on this book, only to be left with nothing. I couldn't see any way to improve the problem and it felt like the entire book was self-destructing in front of me, like my actual computer was on fire. I was in such a swarm of all the beliefs about myself and my ability to write that I couldn't see clearly. All I could see was my nightmare come to life.

Having cried it out, within a few days I found the solution: a job for the love interest that my unconscious had been hinting at all along. I couldn't see what was right there in the text I had written myself because I was too caught in the terror that I didn't know what I was doing.

IN THE YEARS SINCE, I've seen many students and clients hit this point. It takes many forms, from soggy gray clouds smothering you from above, to a moment yelling

"What do you want from me?" at the wall by your desk where the outline of scene cards hang.

Remember that this moment, like all nightmares, is temporary. Don't make any decisions when you're in its grip. It feels like an epiphany that everything is a disaster and can't be solved, but it will shift. When appearing on the Secret Library Podcast, author V. E. Schwab shared that every time she reaches this point in a novel, she emails her agent and says she wants to hold down the delete key on the entire book. It feels like an entirely new level of despair each time.

"Oh, you're at that point again?" her agent replies. When she protests that this is a new level of disaster, her agent forwards a nearly identical email from the previous novel, claiming similar levels of hopelessness. We believe that our inability to get through this moment is unique, but it isn't. Not even within our own writing lives.

The nightmare is a bit like the Tower in the Major Arcana, another card people often hate pulling. It feels like all is lost, but hitting this low point allows us to drop what isn't working. It truly wasn't possible for me to complete the novel if the love interest had no job or life goal of his own. But that being true didn't mean there was no hope for the book.

As with all the fears that come with the Swords, the way through this card is, once again, to separate the useful concepts from the howling despair.

———

THE QUESTION **of the Nine is this: What am I making this mean?**

THE FEARS of the Eight are an accumulation of all the scariest beliefs we have about ourselves and our abilities. If they continue unchecked, they glom onto anything that isn't working in the book and become the nightmare of the Nine.

In my example, the fact that the story had deflated when a main character had no driving force created the nightmare of "I'll never finish this book, I knew I couldn't make it, I can't create a satisfying story arc and no one will ever want to read this." We make small things mean the worst result possible when in the nightmare.

There was a piece of the story that wasn't working, but the nightmare appeared when I allowed the critic to tell me why it wasn't working. A helpful assessment would have been, "This character having no job is killing the momentum. Let's revisit that because it's clearly a very important aspect of the book, more essential than I realized."

Nightmare assessment: "You have written a terrible book that's a total disaster because you don't know what you're doing and the whole thing is going down in flames. Your life as a writer is over."

You'll be able to spot the nightmare by its extreme position. There is no perhaps, maybe, or any kind of qualifying language in a nightmare. It pours out like a prophecy that has already been carved into the stones of time. It isn't.

However, it takes time to wake up from the dream of believing the worst. With the nightmare, you will likely need the equivalent of a really bad night to come out the other side. If you find yourself crying, raging, doubting or in despair, this is ok. Take comfort in knowing you're not alone.

EVERY WRITER HAS their nightmare moment. This always reduces the level of panic I feel when it arrives. At this stage, it's welcome, because there is almost always a breakthrough soon after this night of horrors passes.

Once you're ready, separate the challenge you're facing in the writing from what you're making it mean to see the way through. In my case, a plot element not working didn't mean I was never going to finish that or any book. It didn't mean I was no longer a writer. It just meant I had to make a decision about the story to finally solve the issue.

Nightmares often feel silly once you come out the other side. They aren't. The experience of the fear is real. Be gentle with yourself, and the sun will return for a better morning afterward.

QUESTIONS TO PONDER:

- What is your nightmare about your book?
- What beliefs are building up that you haven't yet investigated?
- What feels too scary to confront?

- Are there any monsters lurking under your writing desk?

33

TEN OF SWORDS

FROM TIME TO TIME, life pulverizes us. We fight and fight and still, there is nothing left to give. If the nightmare has come and you were unable to wake from its horrific images, you may end up here, where everything seems completely hopeless.

The Ten of Swords is possibly even scarier than the Nine. It is depicted with a figure collapsed on the ground, ten swords stabbed along its backbone. Whereas with the Nine of Swords we are wild-eyed and terrified, at this point the thoughts are much shorter: I can't. I'm done.

This point is as bad as it gets, which is the good news. You have reached the point of surrender, and sometimes that's where we need to go in order to learn we can survive. I often think of reaching the end of the Swords like Alice in Wonderland falling down the rabbit hole to the bottom. At first, we scramble to try to get back out the top, but eventually it can be easier to sink all the way down, watching the fears as we go. Only then can we exit the nasty spiral through the door into the garden.

. . .

ONCE YOU BECOME afraid you absolutely cannot do this, stop fighting. Try watching the fears pass by like Alice watches the items on the shelves inside the rabbit hole. There's no need to struggle. You're almost at the bottom. And once you hit the floor and the fears get quieter, it's time for a pause. This is the dark night of the soul, perhaps even more than the nightmare when we're still jumpy and poised to fight off attacks.

Surrender. This too shall pass.

This can come at many points in the writing process. Perhaps you had a nasty experience in a workshop and felt one too many cuts from people's feedback. Perhaps you made the mistake of reading the comments in online forums after your book was published. We can take just so many swipes before it becomes too much. Let go of the fight. You'll find your mind goes quiet and you crave rest. Follow that impulse.

NOT EVERYTHING WILL FEEL like this forever. I've seen people hit Ten of Swords level when they get a detailed editorial note that suggests significantly reworking a manuscript. They read through it, think they can't, and shove it in a drawer, certain they aren't up to the challenge. It's often a huge surprise to them to realize days or weeks later that actually, they are.

The you who can't deserves a rest. The you who's taken too many hits needs TLC. But this isn't the only you who will ever exist. Remember a time when you were very sick. I used to get debilitating throat infections, sometimes for weeks at a time, well into my thirties until I finally convinced a doctor to take my tonsils out. Running boiling fevers and unable to focus, I felt like I had glass shards in my throat every time I swallowed. I most certainly could not do anything then.

Ultimately, I recovered from these bouts of illness. I was not the person who couldn't get out of bed anymore, and I was in a new place. However, the only way I could shift from being ravaged by illness to being able to recover was by surrendering completely and giving it time to pass. Those with chronic illness know this cycle well, with days that feel better than others without any clear reason for the difference. Sometimes we just have to let go. Writing is the same.

As we've learned throughout the Swords suit, all the fears we face here live in your mind. They aren't real monsters you can touch and see. They exist in the little voice that mutters to you, or in the internal monologue that, upon closer inspection, was internalized from another source.

Anne Lamott put it this way, in an article for *Salon*: "My mind is a bad neighborhood I try not to go into alone." When things look this dire, you may need backup. While taking a pause to rest and reset, seek out replenishing input. Perhaps this looks like talking to writing friends, or perhaps it means connecting with a virtual advisor by reading favorite books or watching beloved films. I find author journals and biography hugely helpful in these moments. It's so easy to believe you're the only one who feels it's impossible to get through a struggle with a project. But the more authors I interview and the more of their stories I read, the more certain I am that hitting the Ten of Swords isn't a sign of failure. It's inevitable. We all hit a wall. The question is what we do next.

If you end up here, crumpled on the floor without hope, perhaps you'll be more open to a new approach now, one you've never considered before. What if you cut that one plot thread and combined those two characters? Would that create something new and exciting?

Often we can't see these possibilities until everything has gone up in flames. Once we're willing to throw the whole thing out, we're more open to cutting a part to save the whole.

Ask yourself what you're willing to change to make the project work. We are never more attached to our original concept of a book than right at the beginning. We want that final text to reflect exactly what we'd hoped for. But as we write, we learn new things. We make discoveries and the entire concept may shift into something that's ultimately more satisfying. When we're still in two minds about this, it's hard to let go. The Ten of Swords collapse can be exactly what it was for Alice: a portal to a new world.

It's not that the challenge ends here. Once Alice exited the tiny door and found herself in a sunny garden, she still had to face the Queen of Hearts. But she wasn't trapped in a free-fall forever. Neither are you.

Today may feel impossible. That's ok. Surrender when you can't. Rebuild your energy and restore your peace of mind and, with time, you'll see a way forward. Trust that you'll find your way through.

QUESTIONS TO PONDER:

- Where do you feel you just can't?
- What do you need to surrender for the moment?
- How do you feel like you're in a free-fall?
- What would happen if you let go of trying for the next few hours or days?

34

PENTACLES OVERVIEW

THE MOST CONCRETE of the suits, the Pentacles show us our fears related to tangible results and impact in the physical world. In addition, this suit unearths our fears related to money and compensation for our work.

Whereas the fears for the suits up to this point feel like hovering anxiety, mental chatter, or emotional overwhelm, the Pentacles ground us in fear that directly impacts our everyday lives. With the Cups, you might have wondered how you'd muster up enough energy and enthusiasm to write your way through a whole book. With the Pentacles, the fears about paying bills and organizing schedules arrive. On the flip side, you can also find fears about what might happen if you're too successful with a sudden bestseller on your hands. As we've seen in other suits, our fear isn't only about failures.

Beyond this, we also see fears about the actual craft of writing. Again, these aren't hovering "Am I good enough?" sorts of fears; these fears ask if the sentences are constructed properly, if you've used too many adverbs, or if you'll ever say the thing you set out to write as clearly as you hoped.

WE END with the Pentacles because these fears often contain the ones that came before. As we work through the shades of anxiety and doubt a writer experiences, we begin to separate from those beliefs. You are not the fear that hits you when you tackle a challenging scene or imagine your book in the hands of a reader. All writers experience these moments.

Through the final ten cards, see if you find links between these experiences of fear and the ones that came in previous suits. They collaborate to create a web of resistance, and the more you track how they connect, the easier it is to break free.

In addition, every character you write struggles with these fears alongside you. Your experiences are fuel for writing moments and scenes that will resonate with readers because they feel real. You have been building the tangible experience you need to write complex characters all along, just by showing up and paying attention.

Let's explore the fears of the Pentacles.

35

ACE OF PENTACLES

THE FOUNDATION. The first stone laid. The beginning. Pentacles, also known as Coins or Discs, represent the physical and practical considerations of writing a book. When the idea first pops into your mind, the corresponding fears are about practical aspects of getting it on the page.

Will there be enough time? Is this a waste of the time and energy I have? Fears about being able to make space in your schedule and concerns about what practical sacrifices a book might require all show up.

Often, when people have an idea for a nonfiction book related to something they teach, I've seen them go round and round asking if a book is the most practical form to share that material. "Will I earn more from a course or a workshop than a book?" they ask themselves, as writing this book is a part of their business and, therefore, their livelihood.

. . .

IN SEASON ten of the Secret Library Podcast, we focused on writing and money as the theme, and many issues related to the Ace of Pentacles appeared there. The concern about whether or not we can expect to ever make money from writing a book arrives here. As does the concern about what we're investing. In one interview that season, I spoke to former *New York Times* columnist and financial advisor, Carl Richards, who reminded me that it's not just about money when we're considering a practical decision, it's also about all the resources we have: time, attention, and expertise/skill as well as money that we have to invest in any writing project.

Putting so much of ourselves into an idea is scary because by deciding to write the book, we are taking time, money, attention, and the application of our skills away from other possible uses. We're making a choice to put writing before other pursuits and we ask ourselves if this project will be worth it.

At this point, the best way to sort through these fears is to get clear about what "worth it" means for us. There is no one answer to the question, "What would the book being worth it look like?" Every person will answer differently and you might even answer differently depending on the phase of life you're in or even what kind of year you anticipate having.

WHEN YOU LOOK at the question of worth, explore as many facets as possible. Don't just consider potential financial reward. Consider the creative satisfaction and the emotional and intellectual rewards. Look at how this might impact your community as well as your role in your profession. What results in each of these areas would mean writing the book was an excellent investment of time, energy, attention, and money? Even if you aren't actively spending money to write the book, you may be taking time and attention away from other money-making endeavors, or you may need support at some point, in the form of childcare or book-related services like editing, proofreading, or attending trainings or conferences.

Once you can visualize a successful outcome in each of these areas, rank them in order of importance. Which results are essential and which ones are nice to have? If it's absolutely a must for your book to position you as a bestselling author, but you don't care so much about being groundbreaking in the area you write in, then studying successful story convention in your genre and looking at bestsellers that already exist is a good next step. By contrast, if what makes a book feel worth it is taking on a huge intellectual challenge and huge sales are less of a priority, then researching groundbreaking work and looking at the puzzle of breaking convention will be more helpful than studying how your book could sell the most copies.

These opposing examples show the wide range of priorities writers can have for their books. Always ask yourself more questions about what you want the result to look like until you have a picture so vivid you could step right into it. It's easy to get trapped by terms like "successful" without defining what they mean for us. Even bestseller is vague: one person's benchmark for being a bestseller might be ten times the amount of sales that another author hopes for. Having this level of detail helps you make choices that lead to the goal you actually want to achieve, rather than in its vague direction, not sure of what you actually want.

AS WE'VE SEEN, fears are more frightening when they stay amorphous. The Pentacles lose their grip on you especially quickly once you define what you want clearly. The more specific and tangible your goals are, the harder it is for the critic to hijack the anxiety that can appear in the realm of the practical Pentacles.

When countering fears in the realm of the Pentacles, concrete data is your friend. When you start to fear you don't have enough time, track your time to see where it's going and if that's an accurate assessment of the situation. If you're worried a book won't make you any money, ask yourself what minimum amount of money would achieve your financial goal. Everything above that is a bonus.

Any way to take the fear out of your head into a measurable form will help you calm this fear of not having sufficient resources to complete the book. Many financial planners report that people often believe that their dreams are unattainable because they don't have enough money. However, once people write those dreams down and clarify how much it would cost to reach them, most people realize they are a lot closer than they think.

Your critic may tell you that you don't have enough time or bandwidth to write your book. This can be a way to postpone that dream or even shut it down entirely. But until you've investigated and looked at how much time you actually have available and which resources and support you need, please don't assume it's impossible.

THIS BOOK WAS WRITTEN in an hour a day, five days a week. When traveling or during a few busy periods or when I got sick, I didn't manage five writing sessions those weeks. And yet, the book is still here. Figure out what time and energy you have available. Clarify what would make you feel optimistic forging ahead with the resources and support you've identified as necessary. Ask for what you need and get started. Once you follow through with that plan, you'll have the book in your hands before you know it. This is the power of the Pentacles.

QUESTIONS TO PONDER:

- What resources do you need to write this book?
- What tangible rewards are you imagining the book will create?
- What consequences for your time and energy will this cause?
- How can you address these concerns practically, in detail?

36

TWO OF PENTACLES

MOST OF US begin writing without the luxury of being able to focus on it full-time. Writing gets snuck into corners and moments between other responsibilities. As your momentum builds, carve out more time wherever you can. Some people get up early in the morning before another job. Others write when the kids are napping, or type into phones while commuting on transit or dictate in the car. It's always a juggling act, which is the image associated with the Two of Pentacles.

Balancing writing with other responsibilities brings up the fear that we can't do it all. We fear we'll drop one of the parts of our life we're trying to keep going: writing or living. In reality, it isn't just two things we're balancing. We are spinning plates, with kids, partners, jobs, housework, friends, and more to manage. The ability social media gives us to compare ourselves to others online who seem to spin their plates effortlessly doesn't help.

. . .

MANY WOULD-BE writers worry that taking writing seriously will lead to dropping those precariously spinning plates, shattering them all. Writing does take time away from other responsibilities. These chunks might be short, thirty minutes at a time or even less, stolen from other activities, or a whole day if that's how you prefer to work. Trusting that the plates won't crash when you turn your attention to writing takes preparation and commitment. More than one of my clients begin our sessions dreaming of more writing time but bemoaning the reality that their schedules won't allow the. But is this entirely true? One client fantasized about four days a week for writing and was ready to give up on taking more time at all. Once we looked closely at her schedule, we found that she could dedicate two and a half days a week without compromising other commitments. The critic was so scared that plates would get dropped if she gave writing any more time that it took slowing down to find the real time that could be made available.

We fear putting anything down because we believe so strongly that we need to keep juggling and balancing everything ourselves without asking for help. If we can manage those plates, then we don't get to write. The antidote to this fear is not getting better or more efficient at juggling responsibilities. We need to go a bit deeper to escape.

THE FEAR HIDING under the knowledge that you can't manage everything is the belief that real writers do it alone and never need help. This is absolutely untrue.

Grab any book you have on hand and turn to the acknowledgments section. There is most often a small army behind the scenes of any published book, traditional or independent, and without that support the book simply wouldn't exist, from editors to designers to encouraging loved ones.

Part of finishing your book is creating structures and systems that allow you to step away from your spinning plates. This will feel scary at first, perhaps even reckless. Stick with me. Assess what time and space you need to devote to the book and weigh it against the responsibilities you currently have. Does that amount of time exist in your schedule? No, it doesn't count if you choose to give up sleep. Who do you need to talk to about freeing up the time you need? Whose help do you need to free up time away from the plates so you can write, even if it's just for short sessions to begin with?

This might be a babysitter a few hours a week, or it might be teaming up with other writing friends to rotate running a play group so the other parents can write while one watches the kids. This might look like exploring a flex-time schedule at work or simply actually taking lunch breaks to write outside of the office instead of eating at your desk.

TO BEGIN, watch your schedule for a week. Note down how you spend your time in 30-minute increments or smaller units of time, if you can. Look at what you are spending your time on and whether you are ok with those allocations. What help would be required to keep everything going if you stepped away a few times to write? This won't be a perfect system at first, and compromise is often necessary. Maybe a whole day isn't possible, but two half-days on weekends are. Creativity comes into all parts of writing, even the planning and organization of your schedule. As with my client above, don't let the critic talk you out of the time you can spend just because it doesn't perfectly match your dream schedule.

THIS IS AN ONGOING PROCESS. You don't need to get this perfect, and sometimes a plate will fall, maybe even shatter, as you settle in and establish your new routine. This happens in all aspects of life, so don't take it as a sign that you shouldn't be writing. Yes, there are plates we absolutely cannot let break, like the safety of those in our care, but running late once or forgetting something at the grocery store happens to everyone. Be gentle with yourself and remember that this is a work in progress.

There is no perfect system nor a perfect schedule. There are a lot of books and articles that claim to offer this, but I haven't found a golden ticket. You will always need to tweak and adjust. Juggle the juggling, so to speak, because even when you hit your stride, something will change and you'll have to adjust again. Seasons change, flu outbreaks come, someone goes on leave at work shifting responsibilities, and so on.

. . .

THE BEST WAY TO balance well is to ask for help when you can't spin any more plates. To prevent burnout, ask for help before you get overloaded. If you feel ok about how everything is balanced right now, start setting boundaries against taking anything else on. We often live one stomach bug away from collapse.

Finally, remember that it isn't the end of the world to pause your writing when life throws a curveball. A client recently messaged me to say her partner had been rushed to the hospital for surgery and that as a result, she was setting writing aside for the moment. Of course this was the right choice in that moment. You get to choose where you attention is most needed and that won't be with writing one hundred percent of the time. That doesn't make you less of a writer. It makes you a human with real-life experience, and that is just as important as your writing.

Take care of yourself and your loved ones. Ask yourself if you could thrive more with support, and get creative about asking for what you need. This doesn't have to cost more money, but sometimes investing in giving yourself more time and energy can transform how much writing you can ultimately do.

WE'RE all juggling alongside you. This is how the writing life works. Only a very small number of authors manage to make writing their full-time paid work. For the rest of us, writing is part of a system that includes various jobs. This isn't a temporary state — this is the writing life for most of us. Build a strong system that flexes when life throws new plates at you to spin, and you will be able to write through all the complex phases of life, adapting to changes as you need to, without giving up.

QUESTIONS TO PONDER:

- What responsibilities are you currently juggling?
- Which plates need to be kept spinning, no matter what?
- Who can you ask for help?
- What tasks can you let go of for the moment?
- How would it feel to say no to any of the items on your calendar?
- What do you need to make more space for writing?

37

THREE OF PENTACLES

FOR EVERY WRITER, there comes a time when you need someone else's eyes on your work. Even if you write alone, after publication, your readers will turn the pages without you present. Despite this being our goal in the first place, huge amounts of fear come up when we imagine anyone else with their hands on our writing.

This can happen at multiple points. Perhaps you've joined a writing group and have to share pages. You may have just sent your book out to a group of beta readers. Or maybe after struggling for a while, you've decided to try working with an editor.

AFTER WORKING on a novel for several years, tinkering with point of view, the span of the story and who told it, I lost motivation to continue. It felt like I was sliding all over a frozen lake, unable to find any traction. When I chanced to interview the writer Simon van Booy for the Secret Library Podcast about his story collection, *The Sadness of Beautiful Things,* I felt a spark. Here was someone who wrote about relationships and the impact people have on each other the way I wanted to. When I gathered links for the show notes, I saw he also offered editing services. I reached out right away.

We met for coffee when I was in New York to see family in late December and spoke about the novel. He understood my characters and the concept right away. We made a schedule and I planned to send him pages in January.

EVEN WITH ALL THIS PREPARATION, as soon as I hit send on those pages, I felt sick. Despite having workshopped the novel before, this felt different. I'd changed the concept, committed to ideas that had felt tentative before. And I was letting someone whose opinion mattered to me read them.

I paced our tiny furnished flat in Berlin, waiting for his feedback. Fear that he'd cancel working with me after reading the excerpt left me shaky until I got his notes. His comments were helpful and positive, but the fears that took over before they arrived were pure Three of Pentacles.

FROM AN EARLY AGE, we defer to teachers for judgment on our work's quality. We get grades, comments, and notes which leave us feeling validated or judged depending on the tone. Rarely, if ever, are we encouraged to sort through someone else's response to our work to find what's truly useful.

This points to the true fear: that someone else gets to decide if you are actually a writer or not. Once readers and editors and potential agents or even well-meaning family and friends look at your work, you may worry about the impact of the response.

Writers spend a huge amount of time working alone, immersed in the world of the book. This can be a satisfying time, but as we've seen through this book, it can also be a time full of fear. The moment when someone else sees what you've been working on can feel like judgment. Was this project worth all this effort? Is this any good?

No one else gets to decide the answer to that question. Everyone has opinions about writing and what they enjoy reading. Know that those you collaborate with may have different opinions when they respond to your writing. Their ideas aren't more valid than yours just because they aren't yours.

THE THREE OF Pentacles depicts three people with different skills working together. Often, the card shows them jointly constructing a cathedral. There may be an artist, an architect, and a stonemason. These three figures want to create something beautiful together, but their opinions about how it should be done are informed by their own experience and skills. It's the same with writing.

If you plan to share your work for feedback, look for someone with the skills you wish to cultivate, but also discuss what input you are looking for before sharing your work. As with this card, the vision of "a cathedral" is too general to ensure that the result will be harmonious. You need to have a concrete goal for the building, including the layout of each portion, the height of the tower, the design of the stained glass, and every feature that's involved in order to successfully co-create the architectural concept you each have in mind.

Similarly, creating a vision for what you want your book to convey and how you want it to land with readers before sharing your pages for feedback helps those supporting you to tailor their feedback.

The most damaging thing you can do to your work — and yourself — is to hand your writing over, asking only the most useless question there is: "Is it any good?" There is no universal good, just like there is no one way to build a cathedral. It's necessary to share your concept with your collaborators, and to define your goal before seeking responses from others.

————

THE QUESTIONS **I ask anyone who I share my work with are the following:**

- What do you think this piece is about?
- What did you like about it?
- Were you ever confused? If so, when and where?
- What were you especially curious about? Did you wish there was more written about this /

would you have hung out longer in any parts of the piece?
- (For fiction) Who was your favorite character, and why?

WHEN COLLABORATING ON A WRITING PROJECT, my wish is that everyone involved understands the project and is equally dedicated to it becoming the best possible version of itself. Once this is clear, you can avoid unhelpful feedback that takes the project in a different direction. When someone doesn't share in the vision of the project, for example if they prefer a different genre, or love a good tragedy even though your story has an uplifting ending, you're not aligned toward creating a book that fully embodies the vision you have for it. This can still happen, even after you have a discussion.

If there is a miscommunication, remember that it's ok to disregard unhelpful feedback. We'll look at more fears related to this through the Pentacles, but for now, return to the statement you made about the vision for the book to ground yourself. If the feedback doesn't serve the vision, you can safely let it go.

Make sure to take space to feel the fears that come up with sharing your writing. Even if you don't incorporate all the feedback, the feelings it brings up are real. Be kind to yourself in these moments, so that sharing and collaborating with others can grow to support you and the book. Together, you can realize the dream you've worked so hard on.

38

FOUR OF PENTACLES

AT SOME POINT in everyone's writing life, this happens: you have an idea that feels like THE ONE. You work on it for a while, but life gets in the way of writing, forcing you to set it aside. Cut to later on, when you're peacefully browsing in a bookshop and there on the shelf is the book you didn't finish. Ugh. What a punch to the gut.

How did they write my book? Why didn't I finish it? That was my idea! The critic kicks into high gear and we are riddled with doubt. What if this was my one good idea and I've wasted it?

THE FOUR of Pentacles is the fear that ideas are scarce. We grasp them, thinking that we'll only have so many in life and that the ideas we have need to be parceled out gradually, for fear of squandering this limited resource. This one kicks in when people read Elizabeth Gilbert's *Big Magic*, which includes the story of a book she set aside during a chaotic year, only to find that the idea had defected to Ann Patchett, ultimately becoming *State of Wonder*. Gilbert even references a moment when she kissed Ann Patchett in greeting as the point when she imagines the idea fluttering into Ann's mind. I don't believe that Elizabeth Gilbert intended to cause writers worldwide to scream inwardly, terrified that setting their writing aside for even a day would leave them destitute, their idea having abandoned them. And yet, I've heard this fear so often that it almost deserves its own book.

THIS SAME FEAR works against us when we make big changes as we revise. After all, the critic points out, we've spent lots of time working on that section, or that paragraph or even, in some cases, that entire plot line. If we cut it, it means we've wasted all that energy. And, perhaps, we've wasted an idea and we won't get another one.

If you look a bit deeper, you'll realize this isn't how ideas work. After all, what happens when you really embrace one idea for a story? Other ideas appear, right? If we ask "what if?" about a character in a certain time and place facing a challenge, ideas flow from that original premise. We don't have to grind through every element of a story and if we do, we start to think this isn't the project for us after all.

WHEN WE OPERATE from fear that there won't be any more ideas and we have to make the most with the scraps we have, we get stingy. You might have a line of dialogue in your head that you love, but if you worry there's no more where that came from, then you'll hoard it like Gollum with his Precious, afraid to ever put it down on the page. This fear is self-fulfilling, because I find whenever I start to hoard an idea, it turns into a blockage that prevents more ideas from coming.

After all, the best way to generate more ideas is to let the current ideas flow. Try them. Write them down. The critic is shutting you down with this idea of scarcity because it is an excellent way to derail the entire writing process. If you hold on to that one idea, you're like a monkey reaching into a cookie jar: so long as you grip onto that one idea, you'll never be able to get your hand back out again. The limited idea fear is a trap.

HUMANS NATURALLY CREATE MEANING in the form of story. Think about how many times we make them up without even trying. Any gap gets filled with plot as explanation. Have you ever waited for a call that didn't come? Explanations flooded your mind the whole time you stared at the phone, right? Whether you were waiting for a date to call again, or an answer about a job, or any other reason we wait for word, we make up stories to explain. We don't stop at one, either, surrendering to not knowing the truth. We come up with explanation after explanation, whether we want to or not, even calling friends to help us generate more stories.

We don't see this as making up stories, though. In our heads, writing is somehow different. We believe that writing ideas are fragile and that generating them is different from every other skill we've learned. We don't run out of things to say in a conversation with a friend, but we believe we'll run out of ideas in our stories. What if that wasn't true?

The sooner we embrace the awareness that there are always more ideas, the easier it is to write. If we let one idea go, another one will be right there behind it, and the more ideas we try, the more will be created by having written and explored the ones we've had on the page, whether we keep them or not.

AT THE LA TIMES FESTIVAL OF BOOKS a number of years ago, Diana Gabaldon pulverized this fear with a single throwaway comment. She discussed various aspects of writing the Outlander series. The interviewer asked how she dealt with history contradicting the timeline in her books. Was she ever tempted to ignore historical detail if it didn't match a storyline she'd already planned?

"They're just words," she said. "I can always write more."

I was stunned. This has become a mantra when I get too grasping about any one idea or scene that doesn't fit when I revisit the draft. If you relate to this fear, this might belong on a sticky note by your desk:

THEY'RE JUST WORDS. **You can always write more.**

. . .

QUESTIONS TO PONDER:

- How would it feel to know the idea isn't everything?
- What if it was safe to take the time you need to write your story?
- Have you read multiple books on similar topics?
- What made you keep reading?
- How were each of these books valuable to you?
- What would change if you knew there was room for your book even if others have written stories with similar elements?

39

FIVE OF PENTACLES

WHILE WORKING ON THIS BOOK, I sent an informal survey question to my Substack community at Book-Alchemy.com:

What scares you most about writing? I'm dying to hear all your fears, *especially* the weird ones.

What came back were lots of fears, but none that I'd call weird. Many remarked on what a relief it was to see others were scared of the same things. And the most common theme of all?

"...nobody cares anyway."

"...the underlying fear is that the writing doesn't resonate with anyone."

"Nobody understanding my humor."

"That it won't find the audience it's supposed to. That it won't mean anything to anyone but me."

"That I'm wasting people's time."

"That I have no idea what is good or what people like."

"What scares me the most is whether people will be interested..."

THE MOST LIKELY fear of all is not about technical skill, but rather that the writer will never feel a sense of connection or understanding from readers. The pain of having put in hours, months, years, without bridging the gap between writer and reader feels devastating.

There's no better image to capture this than the Five of Pentacles, most commonly depicted as a figure out in the cold, separate from the cozy space inside. This card makes me think of the Hans Christian Anderson story of the Little Match Girl, burning out her hopes in the dark, one by one, until she freezes.

The story, when told this way, is truly grim. Living a life never able to feel accepted and supported is enough to break your heart, and without conquering this fear, that may be exactly what happens.

The reframe needed here is a subtle one, and it requires a few steps. The first is to recognize that fearing you won't find a supportive audience isn't the same as knowing that for certain. Just because you're afraid no one will love or understand your story doesn't mean no one ever will. Our first shift is to understand this is the critic trying to convince us it can see the future. This is an impossible undertaking for anyone, making its predictions untrustworthy.

If you worry no one will understand and that you're all alone in a cold world working on this story, how do you respond to this?

IN MOST CASES, I see one of three outcomes:

1. Delaying sharing the work, for fear this will only confirm that no one values it.

2. Trying to get proof that the work will be a success before being willing to share it.

3. Another fear glomming on as this fear's paralysis sets in.

LET'S take them one by one. First of all, these reactions are not shameful or wrong. In fact, they are quite logical. If you believe that sharing your work will prove you've been wasting your time, why put yourself through that? In business, would-be founders seek proof of concept before producing a product at scale, so why wouldn't you try the same with writing? If you're already scared, other messages the critic whispers in your ear can feel louder and more real.

These ways of thinking are flawed, seeking proof that the worst outcome won't happen without a way to confirm a successful result. If you believe that sharing the work will confirm it's been a waste of time, you'll never seek anyone's input. The scary outcome is terrifying enough to that you sacrifice the possibility of support and encouragement, while the work sits in the drawer for years, discarded and forgotten. The negative outcome isn't the more valid one just because it feels scarier.

WE ARE EVOLVED to respond more powerfully to negative feedback because, early in human existence, negative outcomes could be fatal, while positive outcomes were simply nice to have. We haven't yet rebalanced the importance of these two outcomes, and social ostracism and rejection — certain death to cultures facing the elements without our modern conveniences — scare our nervous systems more than almost any other outcome.

This leads me to our second unhelpful approach: In order to risk rejection, we try to forecast the response we'll receive. The problem with this approach is that we are inherently biased about our own work, making us terrible judges. Over the months and years we work on our writing, we become less and less objective. I tell almost all my clients and students who've reached a second or third draft that they are now fired from deciding how engaging and interesting the book is.

PICTURE YOUR FAVORITE BOOK. The one you love most of all, one that kept you up late at night because you were compelled to keep turning the pages, even as your eyelids slid shut. How many times have you read that book? If you're like me, I have beloved books I've read two or three times, and even a few I read annually as part of a tradition. But by the time I'd read them a few times, it was no longer about the book being interesting, it was about revisiting a familiar world where I already knew what would happen. I no longer see the book with fresh eyes, even after two or three readings, even far apart. If we can't manage that with someone else's writing, why would we think we could judge our own words after at a minimum the same number of re-reads?

TO GET a sense of how the work is going, we have to trust someone else. Beyond that, we have to trust ourselves to choose a helpful source of feedback and to let them read our work, listening to what they share, even if we find it painful. We don't have to agree with everything they say, but by seeking input from a trusted source, we learn something important: is the effect we wanted to have on readers is, in fact, the effect we are having? This is not about judging quality — it's about learning how the book is landing with readers.

SADLY, we can never be guaranteed success before we risk writing and sharing the book. We have to shape it into a form we're ready to set free into the world. Unfortunately, we eventually have to throw the book into the void and wait to see where it lands.

This is where other fears sneak in teaming up. I see the Five of Pentacles' "Little Match Girl" clinging to other fears so often, it's like it seeks connection with other terrors, certain it will never find safe warm space and feel loved any other way.

HERE'S how to recognize that two (or more) fears are working together. It feels like a mean gang loitering in your mind, heckling you at every turn. Identifying who is in the gang is the first step, hopefully helped by reading about the fears in this book. List them out and work with each one separately. Having one fear doesn't mean you'll be left in the cold alone.

———

HERE ARE a few examples of paired-up fears:

"The writing isn't good enough, so everyone will reject it."

"I'm bad at grammar, so no one will ever take my writing seriously."

"I've picked the wrong idea, so I'm never going to find readers for this story."

Two fears happening close together doesn't mean that the existence of one proves the other. As we've seen, these fears have their own solutions, as does the fear that your writing, and you as a writer, will never be accepted.

This is a tough one, and while it's simple to say, it's much harder to put into practice. The only way you can get through the fear that your writing will never be accepted is to accept your writing yourself first. If you dedicate yourself to your writing and believe it's worth putting the effort into even if people don't immediately understand it, you will overcome this fear.

IF YOU WANT to work on your books until you've created a version you're proud of and this matters more than what people think, it will no longer be a cold outdoors you find yourself in if the reception isn't what you expected. No one else's opinion can matter more than your own.

This takes years to work through, so as you are making steps to trust yourself, gently questioning the negative assumptions when they come can help keep you going.

WHAT IF NO one ever cares about my work?
  —> What if someone really cares about my work?
  What if no one understands what I'm trying to do?
  —> What if they really, really get it?
  What if there are people who hate this book?
  —> What if there are people who love it?

KEEP PUSHING BACK. Until the book is out in the world, we can't know what the result will be. Even then, the initial response isn't an accurate judge of a book (or any creative work) and its ultimate value. As long as the book exists, there is the possibility for it to help someone. Are you willing to take the risk to ensure someone is able to find it? That choice is entirely yours.

40

SIX OF PENTACLES

"I LIKED IT. It was really good." Ahh, the most dreaded words a writer could receive in response to someone reading our writing for feedback.

To be fair, I am very happy when someone enjoys reading what I write. However, when I've shared a draft for constructive feedback and all I get in reply is "it was good," I panic, which brings us to the Six of Pentacles fear: that everyone is just being nice about your writing.

THIS CARD often pictures a wealthy figure balancing a set of scales to decide which of the figures begging below them deserve their charity. Whenever you receive a compliment about your work, it's very easy to fear that it was only charity.

Stressing about whether people genuinely liked your book is a tough one, because it's very difficult to convince your critic that anyone is expressing real enthusiasm rather than politeness.

Don't run off to hide in the wardrobe shrieking in pain like Moira Rose just yet. There is a way to tackle this one.

PEOPLE GIVE bland feedback because they don't want to cause harm. This is not because they hated your book, but rather due to a lack of guidance about what response would be most helpful. If you ask someone to read your book and then tell you what they thought of it, they have no idea what you're asking for on a practical level.

However, if instead you send them the manuscript along with a note like this:

———

HI JANE,

I'm sending you my manuscript, *Book Title,* as we discussed. Would you please read it and let me know the following:

- What you liked about it
- Any places you were confused
- What parts you wished continued longer
- If you felt the ending to chapter 7 was too abrupt (Insert your own specific question(s) here)

If you have a chance to read this in the next 2-3 weeks and share your thoughts, I'd be most grateful. I'm hoping to start the next draft by [DATE].

Thanks again!
Your name

———

DO you see how this makes it easier to give a useful response with this specific direction? Most people want to be helpful, and in the absence of being useful, they'll do their best not to be unkind.

In our scenario above, where someone simply said, "It's good — I liked it," they were likely trying to be kind, rather than concealing a powerful dislike of your writing. They just didn't know what you need from them.

The world doesn't give out overly generous praise to creatives as a default. In most cases, it's the reverse: work that would delight many readers doesn't get picked up because a publisher isn't sure how to market it.

THE CRITIC IS suspicious of any positive feedback, because it's hard to trust that this enthusiasm is reliable. We never know how long our good fortune will last, so we mistrust praise and overvalue harsh criticism.

After a year working with my editor, whose feedback I was originally terrified of receiving, I noticed a shift in my critic's response to his feedback. "You can't trust his opinion. He's already invested in the book now. He's no longer impartial."

Interesting that my critic latched onto my editor's caring about the book as a liability. But caring in general seems to make the critic suspicious. I've heard of people who don't mind sharing work with strangers, but fear they are just being nice and that close friends and family will judge them if they ever found out about their writing. I've also heard from writers who don't trust their family and friends' positive response, worried that the public in general will tear their stories apart. In almost every case, I watch people care more about the imaginary negative response they haven't even gotten than the positive comments they have.

THE TRUTH IS, not everyone will love your book. I write everything I publish expecting that someone will dislike it. This frees me up to write what I want to share, because success doesn't require that I make everyone happy. In order to keep writing, I have to trust that people will be honest when sharing their opinions.

We are hard-wired to take negative feedback more seriously. Nearly every writer starts out working with me sharing the hope of getting some "really critical" feedback. Interestingly, aggressively critical "no pain no gain" feedback, while perceived as more valuable, almost always does more harm than good.

If a book is working, there is no need to tear it apart to improve it. If you've formed an idea with potential that hasn't yet taken a fully successful shape, wouldn't you rather hear what could work or what the reader is curious about, rather than what they don't like?

Someone sharing what they don't like with no constructive suggestions gives you no useful information to take action on. If you take every comment you receive as equally valid, it's very easy to lose your way. Ultimately, you must decide what a successful final version of your story is. Be careful when you turn yourself into the figure begging from another person, giving them the power to decide if your writing is worth continuing.

THIS IS the flip side of this fear: that anyone who dislikes your book is automatically right. In reality, when I dislike a book, it has a lot more to do with my taste than the skill of the author. No matter how brilliant a writer is, if they are writing in a genre or on a topic that doesn't connect with me, I won't enjoy the book. But my option is no more valid than another reader's who may love the genre or the topic and mark the book among their favorites. If you only get feedback from one person, you are missing the variety of opinions that exist for every book. Don't let the fear of feedback stop you from seeking it from multiple people, once you share your work.

THE THINGS that generally make a book unsuccessful are confusing the reader or boring them. Many readers complain about abrupt endings and unclear storylines. In addition, not trusting the reader to understand a story and info-dumping causes people to disengage. But these are questions you can get helpful feedback about. Select several people to act as early readers, asking more people than you need, as not everyone always gets back to you in a timely fashion. Make sure the readers are fans of the genre you're trying to write. If someone only reads detective fiction, their opinion of your YA romance doesn't help you at all. What they dislike, a true fan of the genre may gobble up. Set yourself up to get useful responses. Don't go looking to get torn apart simply because you're scared your book isn't good enough.

There is no such thing as good enough. However, there is meaningful improvement and that is possible with concrete feedback. Find readers who are a match for your work, ask concrete questions for them to respond to, and you are far less likely to hear the dreaded "I liked it. It was really nice," ever again.

QUESTIONS TO PONDER:

- What are you most afraid of hearing from early readers ?
- What points do you want specific feedback on?
- How would it feel to ask for input on these areas?
- What are you afraid it will mean if people don't understand or connect with your book?

41

SEVEN OF PENTACLES

EVERY SO OFTEN, we must pause to look at how the writing is progressing. This is a critical moment, as our attitude toward our progress determines how satisfied we feel about the project. I'm a firm believer in the notion that each of us has a sweet spot of writing effort.

Whenever I've set aside time for a writing retreat, whether I've been housesitting for a friend, or staying somewhere with the express purpose of writing, it's been tempting to plan for extra-long writing days.

"Wonderful! I'll finally be able to write ten hours a day," we fantasize, but with very rare exceptions, no one I know writes that many hours a day. Even Stephen King, touted as the poster child of the prolific, shares a schedule in *On Writing* that features an afternoon for reading and admin, and evenings spent with family.

ON WRITING RETREATS, I generally write for two hours a day and spend the rest of the time resting or topping up my creative reserves. In order to write two solid hours, there need to be a lot of deep creative inhales. For example, I read twice as much when I'm working solidly on a book, and need to go to bed earlier as well to get as much sleep as my insomniac system can manage.

If we take my two-hour-daily retreat habit and assess my progress, here are a few ways your brain might respond:

I should be writing more!

Most writers start here. You probably have a very long list of what your writing process is *supposed* to look like. This could be a staggering word count per day, numbering in the thousands, or it might be the expectation that you write for as many hours as you might spend in an office at a standard office job.

"I wrote for two hours, but I should have written for eight. Ugh," or, "I wrote 500 words, but I should have written 5,000. UGH," are symptoms of this mindset.

———

WHAT IF YOU **didn't pathologize your progress?**

What if we calibrated our expectations around what was actually doable for us? After all, you likely have things you're responsible for other than writing. You may have children, elderly parents, a full-time job unrelated to writing, and countless other commitments.

If your life is built so an hour a day is what's possible — that's how I wrote this book, as mentioned previously — then why not celebrate that as the ideal outcome?

Fear of not doing enough does so much more harm than good. Somewhere along the line, we learned that beating ourselves up was a virtuous approach. I suspect our inner critics sent this in as a saboteur, because feeling we're not doing a good job is a surefire way to make us want to quit.

———

IMAGINE planning for the doable outcome. Which of these makes you want to continue writing:

"Shit, I only got an hour of writing in today. I need to make more time for this. I'm never going to get anywhere."

"Excellent! I wrote for the hour I set aside today. Right on track."

PAUSING to take stock is most helpful when you reflect not just on the quantity of your output, but also on the quality of your writing experience. It's not necessary to suffer in order to write something meaningful. You're far more likely to write consistently and finish what you set out to accomplish if you feel good about how the process is going.

If you notice that you consistently criticize your pace and are in a "not enough" loop where no amount of time spent writing or pages or chapters or scenes completed feels like enough, it's time to pause.

You don't just want to count out words like coins. Pause and take a breath. Are you winded and worn down? Do you feel like you're barely hanging on as you write this project? If so, it's time to adjust the plan.

WRITING a complete piece of any length is a multi-step project. It's easy to get sucked into believing that the end result justifies a grueling pace. I disagree. Having finished a number of manuscripts at this point, I can report that the experience of getting to THE END is a lot less dramatic than you'd expect.

It feels like blowing through a tiny town in the American Midwest with only one stoplight. By the time we realize we've arrived, we've already blown past the experience.

"Was that it?" I've often thought, finishing the final page. I've seen countless students in live write-along sessions staring at the screen like they've just come out of a dark cinema and got blinded by the sun.

"I think I might have just finished my book?" one said in a study hall, blinking at the end of a novel draft on the screen in front of her. I usually have to convince them that it's time to celebrate now. They weren't ready for the process to be over, stunned that slow and steady actually got the draft done.

————

ENJOYING the writing along the way is the only cure I've found for this anti-climax at the end. Setting a manageable goal and hitting it consistently allows you to combat the gnawing sense of being behind. The only thing you're behind is your beliefs about how you're supposed to be writing.

If you have a pub deal or a contract with a due date, then this is another story. But in that case, it's still essential to plan based on a schedule that isn't going to leave you a husk of your former self. This might involve saying no to other commitments and clearing out your calendar so you can focus on the book. There is no way to increase your energy level while asking more of yourself each day.

Writing a book without a deadline means you get to write it in a way that satisfies you. There is no reason to torture yourself. I've coached enough people at this point to watch them shift from suspicious to delighted as they learn first-hand that a doable goal makes the whole process feel better.

DON'T LET the fear that you're behind shut you down. Embrace what effort you can make as enough, do it consistently, and pause regularly to take in the satisfaction this creates and watch your entire relationship to writing change.

We'll look at how this idea expands into another fear and another way to transform it with the Eight.

QUESTIONS TO PONDER:

- What do you believe is the "ideal output" you *should* be generating?

- How much do you actually tend to write, time-wise or in terms of output (word count or pages)?
- How would it feel to plan based on the output that you realistically and consistently generate?
- Do you enjoy the writing process?
- What would an enjoyable writing process look like for you?

42

EIGHT OF PENTACLES

SKILLS LIKE CARPENTRY, painting and sculpture and spring to mind first with the word "craftsmanship," but we also think of craft with language, word choice and technical writing skills. The Eight of Pentacles is the card that illustrates buckling down on craft.

This, unsurprisingly, is also the point when we begin to fear our skills aren't up to the challenge. Many writers vacillate on whether to get a post-graduate degree. The U.S. is filled with programs that allow adult students to get a Master's in Fine Arts in Creative Writing, and the appeal is strong when you're in the grip of this fear.

DESPITE THE INCREDIBLE expense and time commitment, there is an allure to getting an MFA. "If I have that degree," you think, "I will finally be prepared to write this book." From an early age, we're trained to look for approval from an outside source. We write papers for grades and consider those with letters after their names to be the experts in their field.

BUT THE CORRELATION between degree-holder and published author isn't as straightforward as we'd like to believe. I've had many students and clients show up to work with me having lost the joy of writing because of time spent in an ill-fitting degree program. The competition is staggering, and advanced study can introduce just as many fears as it was meant to assuage.

The fear of never being a good enough writer to be allowed to write a book is one of the most crippling the critic can level at you. It tells you repeatedly that you need to prepare more so that you can write confidently. Unfortunately, the only way to write confidently is to do it often, without despairing when some drafts don't come together right away.

The fear of getting down to work is understandable. We dislike doing things we don't believe we're good at. But just like any other skill, you can improve your writing with practice. To return to our physical art forms mentioned above, the ability to carve a sculpture improves the more you practice. You can handle a brush with more sensitivity the more you paint. Since writing is more abstract, we forget that we need repeated practice creating sentences and paragraphs and pages out of the ideas in our heads in order to feel more skilled at the craft side of writing.

· · ·

AN ADVANCED DEGREE can improve your writing, if only because it requires a student to write a lot. Dedicated time and energy put toward writing is bound to pay off, provided the guidance feels helpful. However, it's important to remember that you can dedicate time and energy to your writing without paying many thousands of dollars to do so.

Given how much of our early lives we follow teacher deadlines and schedules, it's entirely possible you will thrive in an educational setting. But know that the critic's claim that you need a degree to be allowed to write a book is inaccurate. Not only do writers without graduate — or even bachelor's — degrees in writing publish books all the time, many award-winning books we've studied as examples of great writing were written by authors without any formal training.

DEDICATION AND COMMITMENT to writing is the antidote to this fear. If writing is something you love, it's worth spending your time on. Writing that doesn't feel great at first isn't a waste or evidence of your lack of skill. It's an inevitable step in the process. We may know this intellectually, but it bears repeating that the books we read and love have been reworked, revised, edited, and polished over many drafts. The author, and in many cases a team of other people, have worked hard over years to get that book to the state it's in when we read it.

The critic wants you to believe you'll be able to write like that in a first draft if you get enough training. Even worse, it wants you to think you can't write at all if your first draft doesn't hold up to a published author's tenth draft. It's not a fair fight. Even a writer with many published books doesn't write at that level in an early draft. Have they learned things that allow them to write work they're more pleased with sooner? Of course, but writing that reads like someone just wrote it in one go is writing that took months and years of effort.

Clients and students often feel an increase in confidence simply from regular time writing, even in small steps. Before you sign up for a graduate degree, try writing for twenty minutes a day, three or four days a week, and see how your writing develops. Spending time translating the ideas in your head into sentences on the page over and over is the best investment you can make. And if, even after spending that time, you feel the desire to study writing academically, then explore the possibility. But don't make that choice believing it's necessary or required.

Have you ever picked up a book in the library or a bookshop and read it based solely on the author's writing training? Perhaps if it's a book on the writing process you might be curious about their experience. But if you want to read a novel, which do you care more about: the story itself, or the author's degree? I couldn't tell you if any of the novels I've read in the past few years were written by authors with degrees or not. All we can remember is the story, right?

———

AS ALWAYS WITH THE CRITIC, the fear it brings up is vague: I'm not ready to write this. Ask yourself what being ready would look like. Describe your vision of being fully prepared and confident to write this book (knowing that many authors never reach that point until the book is finished).

It's far easier to address individual concerns that are masquerading as a nasty little gang of fears called "I'm not ready." Your gang will be different than anyone else's.

Let's say yours includes the fear "I hate writing description," "I'm afraid this book will be boring," and "I don't know what happens in the middle." Another person's gang of I'm not ready could be "My sentences feel awkward," "I don't know what this character wants," and "I can't get the pacing right." You might both relate to feeling you aren't ready, but the skills you want to improve are completely different. Once you identify the smaller fears that make you believe you need more preparation, you can work on the skills that improve your confidence in those areas as you work through the project.

THIS IS the critic's playbook on repeat: scare you with a vague fear that you can't engage with. Break it down and ask yourself what the next step is, and dive in. You are ready to take the next step. It isn't necessary to be perfect before you start, because if that were true we wouldn't have a single book in the world.

Start now. Confidence appears along the way, when you realize you've been ready this whole time. Address the aspects of readiness that will help you write with more ease once mastered and you'll be writing more confidently —degree or no degree — sooner than you think.

QUESTIONS TO PONDER:

- What areas of writing feel intimidating for me?
- Am I drawn to get an MFA?
- If so, what do I think an MFA degree will provide me?
- Are there other ways to acquire these skills?
- If I do want an MFA, what's my budget and schedule to complete a program?
- What does craft mean to me?

43

NINE OF PENTACLES

THE NINE OF Pentacles is another favorite, and one I confirm the artist has depicted in a way that connects for me before I purchase any new deck. The classical elements include a woman at home in her garden, enjoying the fruits of her labor. This is a beautiful vision, but one with a shadow side.

Every time a writer finishes a book and puts it out successfully, the critic starts to twist the narrative of how it happened. It takes hard work and dedication to keep showing up all the way until the work is done, as we saw in the Eight of Pentacles. And now, we see the results.

However, once we've moved forward in time, the decisions we made, the effort we put in, and the struggles that were part of finishing the book start to fade. It was just luck, the critic says. This last book was a fluke, and you'll probably never be able to pull this off again.

. . .

THIS HAPPENS to every writer who has ever finished at least one book. Remember V. E. Schwab's story of wanting to hold down delete on her book? Most authors freeze up when writing their second novel, even after having a good result with their first. Chloe Benjamin, author of *The Immortalists*, shared in an article for *Poets & Writers* that one of her professors from grad school warned her that people would trash her second novel no matter how good it was. The interaction left her shaken, feeling like writing her second book was just the necessary step to get to the third rather than a meaningful creative endeavor in its own right. But she stuck it out, and we got *The Immortalists* as a result. Turns out, we aren't always doomed.

IT'S essential to remember that your efforts and dedication get you to the end of each book you write. Perhaps you had some serendipitous moments, but you were the one who had to take action on those discoveries. Thankfully, there is a way to counteract the critic's insidious narrative. Without dismantling the fear that your previous success has been a fluke, your beautiful garden can become a prison of accomplishments you think you'll never be able to repeat.

My students groan when I first present this idea, but it's one of the most powerful tools at a writer's disposal: the process journal. What does this mean? Keeping a notebook just for recording your writing process. Before you protest that you already struggle to find the time to write, let alone start another writing-related task, let me assure you that this can be done in two to three minutes at the end of each writing session.

All you need is to dedicate a notebook or document on your computer to record the following:

- The date, time, and location you wrote
- What you worked on
- How it went, both the quantity of work and how you felt about it

THAT'S IT. Many of my students have used a simple five-year diary for this process, using the small space for the current year on the date they work, so you are even spared most of the first step. Notes might look like: *"In Flora's cafe at eleven. Wrote the scene where Jane first meets Lola. Dialogue was a bit awkward, but I got the scene done and will move on to the one where they go to the party tomorrow."*

The gift this gives you happens over time. Because some entries will include, in addition to the sort of details given above sentences like *"UGH nothing was working today. I couldn't get them to leave the house. They just kept blabbing about nothing,"* or, *"I wrote the scene as planned, but it felt wrong. Alex would never say the things I had in mind when I planned the book. Do I need to restructure the whole thing now?"*

· · ·

THIS IS THE GOLD, even though it won't feel like it in the moment. Recording the struggles means you also record the moment when you have an epiphany about why Alex is acting so strange or how to get your characters out of the house, or you understand the leap they need to make and the exact way to set it up. This is what is essential to remember: that writing books is a struggle, but that you're up to the challenge. If you don't record your challenges and your wins, you'll think this time the struggle is too big for you or forget that your previous books were a struggle in the first place.

The critic won't give up just because you're keeping this notebook. It is fighting for its life when you no longer trust its guidance. Truly hilarious things can begin to unfold once you've been keeping your process journal for a while and the benefits begin to surface.

ONE STUDENT'S critic actually tried to convince her that her process journal wasn't an accurate record. She admitted that she once opened it to look back over her experience from a previous draft to see if it was as hard as the revision felt and was shocked to see that it was, despite having no memory of that struggle anymore. "Who is this person who wrote all these notes in here in my handwriting?" she asked me, only half-joking.

Narrative therapy is a branch of psychology that focuses on the stories we tell ourselves about who we are and what we're capable of. We can't possibly remember all the events and moments in our whole lives, so we curate ones that shore up storylines that make sense to us.

. . .

FOR EXAMPLE, we would remember very different moments with a working storyline of "I'm a capable person who can always get through a challenge in the end" versus "I am hopeless and I never figure things out." These are two dramatic examples, but often the process journal helps us counteract the mind's habit of curating memories for an unhelpful narrative, such as "I don't know what I'm doing." Perhaps writing a book is a new skill, so we aren't fully confident in that process yet, but if you look to other areas of your life, there is plenty of evidence for "I can figure something out, even if it's new." If you've ever driven to a new place and had to figure out the directions (or used a navigation app) to get you there, that is evidence of this new story. As is going to a different city and getting around to places you wanted to go. Or taking on a new responsibility at work, or raising kids who present a new challenge every few days, or even hours.

Cultivating a garden of accomplishment, such as books you've written, can be a beautiful haven to celebrate what you've done, as pictured in the Nine of Pentacles, or it can be a torture chamber, mocking your current efforts. The difference is the story you cultivate about how you got to the point you are now.

I HOPE I've convinced you to start a process journal. And before you worry that you're perhaps too early in your process, let me assure you that if you're in the early days of writing, those moments and discoveries are precious, and will be a beautiful reminder to you later in your writing life. There is nothing more validating than looking back to see how scary the process felt at the beginning, having worked hard at writing and realizing you are now confident in that area. And if you've overcome one hurdle, does it still feel impossible to work through another?

Your garden of success will keep growing as long as you trust you're up to the challenge. If you're driven to write and your stories won't leave you alone, I know you'll find your way.

QUESTIONS TO PONDER:

- What successes have you had in your writing life so far?
- Do any of these successes feel like luck rather than the result of your effort?
- If you dig deeper, can you find the choices that led to your results?
- Have you got a notebook lying around that's been waiting for a job? (Or is there a stationery shop you've wanted an excuse to visit?)
- What details would be helpful to keep track of in a process journal?

44

TEN OF PENTACLES

THERE ONCE WAS a king named Midas, well-known to mythology lovers. He lived in a thriving kingdom with nearly every one of his desires fulfilled. This life was shared with his beloved daughter, but it wasn't enough. When Midas had an unexpected encounter with Dionysus, the god granted him one wish. Midas asked that everything he touched would turn to gold.

We know the rest of this story, as Midas delighted in finally having as much of the precious substance as he could dream of, until he touched his daughter, and his greed transformed her into a lifeless golden statue.

THE TEN OF PENTACLES is often called the Midas card, and most see this as a hugely positive draw. We also have the expression "the Midas touch" for anyone who creates prosperity easily. However, these interpretations leave out the moral the king learned: that seeing everything as a source of gold is as much of a curse as it is a blessing.

When we need every story we touch to become a source of gold, the relationship to story changes. This fear embodies the potential shift when a hobby becomes a career: the joy in creating suddenly secondary to paying the bills. Our Ten of Pentacles fear is writing ceasing to be a source of joy because there is now too much riding on our efforts.

BEYOND THIS, we can look at the tragedy of Midas and his daughter to discover another facet of this fear. There are many myths about writers, from the impoverished novelist in the attic apartment to the alcoholic who can't contain all the feeling roiling inside them. Taking these a step further, we find the myth of the writer who views all relationships and experiences as merely material. In other words, we fear that we'll care more about a good story than the person who shares it with us. There is some truth to this — most writers I know are shameless eavesdroppers, as am I, and draw from life to infuse story with genuine emotion. But most writers have a line they won't cross, despite the fear that making a living from writing would pose a danger to holding those boundaries in our personal lives.

We believe the Midas touch will destroy our ability to sense what's ok to write about and what would hurt someone to share. This idea causes many writers to hold back for fear of going too far, destroying their relationships, leaving rejected by all their loved ones due to their writing.

NO ONE ever said the critic wasn't melodramatic, right? Most of my personal fears start with a reasonable concern that quickly escalates to my being ostracized from human society, living on a rocky landscape open to the elements with no way home. As always, the critic lacks the ability to understand nuance.

The Midas touch is all or nothing: once his hand makes contact, gold replaces what was there before, seemingly forever. But the story has another act: staring at the statue that used to be his daughter, the king understands that Dionysus was correct to warn him about this wish. Midas begs for his new power to be removed. The god sends him to wash his hands in the river Pactolus, which removes the curse and thankfully returns everything, included his beloved daughter, to its original form.

MOST OF US forget this part of the story and think everything is ruined if we make a choice that feels wrong. However, if you sense you've gone too far and everything is feeling like a source of gold rather than a meaningful connection, it's possible to reverse course. As with all aspects of writing, this is an experiment, and you'll never learn what works for you until you explore options and discover how they feel to you.

The antidote to this fear is to try writing from personal experience and see where the line is for you.

Write using your life experience and see what feels safe, and what doesn't. The novelist Huma Qureshi does a beautiful job looking at this theme in her novel, *Playing Games*. The main character, a playwright, overhears an argument between her sister and brother-in-law. The sisters' relationship is complicated to begin with, but the complications spiral once the playwright decides to use a few overheard lines from the fight verbatim in her next play. Despite forming entirely fictional characters around the original dialogue, the seed of the play feels like a theft, and she struggles with leaving the lines in versus weakening work she's thrilled with if she takes them out.

ONCE AGAIN, you're left with trusting your instincts and your gut. As you've seen in the fears throughout this book, the critic assumes you can't be trusted to make a good decision. That if you are up against these challenges, you are destined to fail. But the Midas touch is no longer a curse if you make it a chance to re-evaluate your priorities. All these fears are the change to reconsider, to check in, and to make decisions based on what you find.

FEAR ISN'T A DONE DEAL; it's an alarm — a call to pay attention. Something is not right, and the consequences may be dangerous. But the alarm comes before the danger has gone too far. You still have choices. If you trust yourself to act carefully and to consider your options, then fear becomes a gift and an ally to steer you toward a more satisfying outcome and escape the burning building.

Hold the fears we're discussed as lighthouses that show you where the rocks are. This mentality takes time to adjust to. Fear isn't a pleasant experience. We react dramatically: we freeze, we flee, or we attempt to placate and change the reality causing the fear so it goes away. But the more we can take a breath and make space to feel the fear and ask questions about what it's trying to show us, the more we learn.

The first step is to remember that fear is a messenger. At first, you'll run away when it shows up. Simply try to notice what happens when fear arrives before you react. Did you go blank? Did you push away from the writing entirely? Did you stop working or decide the project wasn't viable? Notice if you have automatic responses without any time for reflection or consideration. We want to widen the window bit by bit between the moment you feel the fear and when you act in response.

Above all, don't beat yourself up when you notice all this well after the fact. As much as you can, get curious. "Interesting. I was worried that this series was just a potential income stream and not creative, so I just pushed it away. Hmmm." It will take time to notice these reactions. In the beginning of shifting your mindset, they'll come to you days or weeks later. That's ok. It can help to look back over any reactions you remember from the past now that you have a sense of what to look for. Ask yourself how you might have handled them differently now.

Try not to make yourself wrong for having these reactions. They are understandable if you think you're in danger or about to make a terrible mistake. But as we see in the Midas myth, you can change your mind, wash your hands of the approach that wasn't working, and begin again.

Trust yourself to notice what's happening, and to build a new relationship with fear. I was tempted to title this book *Writing with Fear*, but I changed it, as I worried that title would be too scary. Most of us want fear to go away. I hope you feel differently now.

By writing through your fears, without shutting them down, you stand to find a story that feels closer to the one you dreamed of. Fear is your partner in this process, an advisor that will keep you from hitting the rocks. When fear can speak directly, when you build a relationship with it, you don't have to wrestle with the critic's catastrophic interpretations about what is going on.

WHAT IF YOU were good at assessing what was best for you? What if you could be with fear as it came up and reflect on a new course that took this information into account? This is the gift you receive when you listen to your fears rather than shutting them out.

After all, we don't think all is lost when we see a lighthouse through the storm. We feel relief because it's giving us a point of reference to navigate by before we crash onto the rocks. It will take time, but building this new relationship with fear will allow you to travel safely, even through territory that might have felt too dangerous before.

This is Writing through Fear. May you trust yourself to take this risk and find the stories waiting for you once you begin.

A LETTER FROM THE AUTHOR

Dear reader,

Thank you so much for reading *Writing Through Fear*. I hope it's helped you feel more confident in your own writing.

If you enjoyed this book, please take a few minutes to leave a review. This makes a huge difference in how many people find the book. Even a short review can encourage a new reader to check out a new title.

Leave a review:

Carolinedonahue.com/wtf-review

If you'd like to stay in touch and hear about new releases first, please subscribe to Footnotes here:

Sign up here:

carolinedonahue.com/footnotes

This book came together over my recent years teaching writing and working on my own books. After noticing the

patterns in common fears most of my students experienced, it was my hope that this guide would help writers
feel less alone.

Remember, experiencing fear isn't a sign you're on
the wrong path — it's a sign you're invested and that the
book has the ability to make an emotional impact. Stick
with it! Your writing matters.

Keep going, and keep in touch.

All the best,
   Caroline

REFERENCES AND RESOURCES FOR FURTHER EXPLORATION

Two of Cups

Watch the full series of talks by Ira Glass on Storytelling, which includes the quote included in this chapter.

Rilke, Rainer Maria. *Letters to a Young Poet*. W.W. Norton & Company, 1993.

Three of Cups

Burkeman, Oliver. *Four Thousand Weeks*. Picador Paper, 2023.

Jack, Richard Morton, *Nick Drake: The Life*. Hachette Books, 2023.

Moyes, Jojo. *Me Before You*. Penguin Books, 2016.

Six of Cups

Tharp, Twyla. *The Creative Habit*. Simon & Schuster, 2006.

Seven of Cups

Hall, Alexis. *Glitterland*. Sourcebooks: Casablanca, 2023.

Eight of Cups

McSweeny's Issue 36 (McSweeny's Quarterly Concern). McSweeny's Publishing, 2011

Secret Library Podcast, Season 3:: Episode 4: Containing the Story with Rachael Stephen

Ace of Wands

Interview with Jacqueline Winspear on the Oh! Murder Podcast

Three of Wands

Lamott, Anne. *Bird By Bird: Some Instructions on Writing and Life*. Knopf Doubleday, 1995.

Four of Wands

Secret Library Podcast, Season 1:: Episode 47: Cory Doctorow on Walkaway and the Future of Publishing

Six of Wands

Franzen, Alexandra. *So This Is the End*. TMA Press, 2022.

Eight of Wands

Ferris, Joshua. *Then We Came to the End: A Novel*. Back Bay Books, 2008.

Kleon, Austin. *Steal Like an Artist*. Workman Publishing, 2012.

McCarthy, Cormac. *All the Pretty Horses*. Vintage, 1993.

Rooney, Sally. *Normal People*. Crown, 2020.

Ten of Wands
MYM Writing Lab
Ace of Swords
Katie, Byron, *Loving What Is*. Harmony, 2021.
Three of Swords
Anatomy of a Fall (Anatomie d'Une Chute), Le Pacte, 2023.
KCRW's Bookworm, November 9, 2006. Interview with Zadie Smith, hosted by Michael Silverblatt.
Four of Swords
Cameron, Julia, *The Artist's Way*. TarcherPerigree, 2016.
Five of Swords
Beck, Martha, *The Way of Integrity*. Open Field, 2022.
Six of Swords
Storr, Robert, *Philip Guston: A Life Spent Painting*. Laurence King Publishing, 2020.
Seven of Swords
Flood, Alison,"Romance Novelist Cristiane Serruya accused of plagiarism," The Guardian, February 20, 2019.
Kuang, R.F., *Yellowface*. William Morrow, 2023.
Eight of Swords
Japaridze, Nino. *Japaridze Tarot*. U.S. Games Systems, 2014.
Tools for transcription:

- Otter.ai
- Descript.com
- Google docs

Nine of Swords
Secret Library Podcast, Season 1:: Episode 38: V.E. Schwab on Writing through Fear
Ten of Swords
Lamott, Anne, "My mind is a bad neighborhood I try not to go into alone." Salon, March 13, 1997.
Ace of Pentacles
Secret Library Podcast, Season 10:: Episode 7: Profit Equals Permission with Carl Richards
Three of Pentacles
Secret Library Podcast, Season 1:: Episode 119: How to Write a Good Story with Simon Van Booy
Four of Pentacles

Gilbert, Elizabeth, *Big Magic*. Riverhead Books, 2016.

Seven of Pentacles

King, Stephen, *On Writing*. Scribner, 2020.

Ten of Pentacles

Qureshi, Huma, *Playing Games*. Sceptre, 2023.

ACKNOWLEDGMENTS

So many thanks, first and foremost, to my clients and students who trusted me to bring tarot into the writing space we created together. Special thanks to the participants in the Quarantine Writers Retreat, Dream to Draft, Coffeeshop Writers Group, and all of my individual clients for coaching and literary tarot.

I'm so grateful to Liz Dexter of Libro Editing, whose eagle eye makes my writing look polished. Any remaining errors are mine alone.

So many thanks to Jessica Bell for another stunning cover for the series.

Thank you to those who've shared the brilliant marriage that is tarot and writing, from Theresa Reed, Joanna Penn, and J. Thorn, to the wonderful Footnotes subscribers who were willing to read the book and share reviews all over the internet.

Many thanks to Secret Library podcast listeners, who've found their way to this book. Thank you for listening and for reading.

Thanks to my friends and family who believed in me as I wrote this book and dealt with my complaints about admin and the tech side of writing, to Hugo, Clyde, and occasionally Drakula, who took shifts in my lap purring so I had to keep writing.

Thanks to B for all the warm teas and for understanding about many days I couldn't watch a show or do much more than melt into a heap at the dinner table.

It takes a village to finish a book, and I'm so lucky to have this village. Thank you for reading this book and for being a part of this story.

ABOUT THE AUTHOR

Caroline Donahue is an American writer, book coach, and podcaster living in Berlin. She is the creator and host of the award-winning The Secret Library Podcast and has taught creative writing to hundreds of students and private clients. She holds a Master's Degree in Psychology and Expressive Arts.

She has been reading tarot since 1996 and has been offering Literary Tarot Readings for writers since 2016.

Visit her online at carolinedonahue.com

instagram.com/carodonahue
youtube.com/@CarolineDonahue